Combating Terrorism and Human Rights Issues

Combating Terrorism and Human Rights Issues

Dr Vijay Pal Singh

KALPAZ

First Published, 2020

Published by

Kalpaz Publications
C-30, Satyawati Nagar,
Delhi – 110052
Ph.: 011-47034999, 9811692060
www.kalpazpublications.com
E-mail: kalpaz@hotmail.com

Printed at: G. Print Process, Delhi

Cataloging in Publication Data—DK
Courtesy: D.K. Agencies (P) Ltd. <docinfo@dkagencies.com>

Singh, Vijay Pal, *Dr.*, author.
Combating terrorism and human rights issues / Dr Vijay Pal Singh.
pages cm
ISBN 9789353242480 (HB)

1. Terrorism—Prevention—Law and legislation—India.
2. Terrorism—Prevention—Law and legislation. 3. Human rights—India. 4. Human rights. I. Title.

LCC KNS4352.S56 2020 | DDC 344.5405325 23

Contents

Preface

No day passes by when we do not hear three words, 'Terror' 'Terrorists' and 'Terrorism.' The menace of terrorism has a far-reaching and penetrative effect on society and has an unpredictable nature. It has engulfed the entire world under its clutches, and each one of us is affected due to this menace directly or indirectly.

With the development and progress in the field of science and technology not only the general people are getting benefitted but terrorist organisation are also using new scientific inventions and technologies to upgrade themselves, and are becoming more sophisticated than before. They are endeavouring to acquire the Weapon of Mass Destruction (WMP) and using Information Communication Technology (ICT) meticulously not only to execute their plans but also to widen their network.

The menace of terrorism strikes the very core of human rights. The environment of fear created by terror groups has affected the basic principle of democracy. The treacherous act of terror violates human rights, such as the right to life and liberty, the right to live without fear, among other rights. Thus, urgent, collective and befitted action is required from the States to combat this menace and to restore peace and harmony in the world.

However, all the civilised nations recognised the universality of the phenomenon of terrorism and its inhumane effects, yet surprisingly there is no single consensus definition of terrorism recognised by these civilised nations. Even though the world community acknowledges the inhumane nature of terrorism, there is no specific international convention on terrorism adopted by the world body. Though steps have been taken at both national and international level to combat terrorism, countering terrorism at the cost of jeopardising human rights of people is uncalled-for. Several countries, including India in the name of combating terror enacted laws which are against the well established democratic principles and human rights.

The book intends to inform, speculate, and stimulates further inquest and discussion on the area of counter-terrorism laws and human rights at national as well as international level, and what is written in this book is not be considered as the last word. Ratiocination will come from the reader of the book.

Acknowledgements

Any venture can never be accomplished alone. I extend the gratitude to one and all who encouraged and unselfishly extended their support in publishing this book. I am indebted to number of persons for their time and invaluable suggestions.

The publisher-author association is essential in completing work smoothly and in time. I am thankful to publisher Kalpaz Publications, New Delhi for promptly publishing this modest work.

I will always be indebted to my family members who have always provided complete care and support to complete this work.

Dr Vijay Pal Singh

Assistant Professor

Indian Institute of Management Lucknow

Chapter - 1

Terrorism

The Meaning of the Term Terrorism

The word terrorism is believed to have been derived from the Latin word '*terrere*', which means 'to tremble'. When this word is combined with the French suffix '*isme*', which refers to 'to practice', it becomes 'to practice the trembling' or to cause or cause the trembling'. The word trembling used by the group of revolutionaries called the Jacobins in France during the French Revolution. The English version of this word as 'terrorism' owes to an Englishman's characterisation of the bloodshed he had observed from afar in France, where the French Revolution was underway.[1] The word, 'Terrorism' after that time referred to as a kind of violent, physical intimidation designed to achieve some objective.

Moreover, such activity was treated as equivalent to extortion under criminal law, but in due course of time, the word terrorist was not used synonymously with extortion. Although terrorists' might indeed be extortionists, it was not assumed that all extortionists were terrorist. According to Burke, terrorists followed a crude ideology, pursuing political change by revolution. Thus, terrorism was tied to ideology, pursuing a political change by revolution. Thus, terrorism was tied to ideology, and politics in a battle waged over power and control.[2]

Throughout the next two centuries, terrorism was used often to describe violence in confrontations, overpower and control around the globe, including labour disputes and violent protest with management and ownership of the means of production; revolutions and armed struggles to overthrow or to achieve independence and statehood from foreign occupier; and violent struggles over supremacy of ideologies, including those of anarchy, syndicalism, socialism, marxism, communism, fascism and capitalism. Terrorism was used to describe the activities of groups like the Industrial Workers of the world, Bolsheviks, and many others. Ideological references for terrorism also extended to religion and began to include the battle waged between Islam and Judaism, between Hindu and Islam, between Christian and Islam. Common element among them was violence or the threat of violence, and this violence or threat of violence was different from the accepted norms or rules of war[3].

Definition of Terrorism

Despite the vast publicity and long history of the phenomenon of terrorism, there is no single comprehensive definition of the term terrorism. More than a hundred definitions of terrorism exist, but none of them is universally accepted. Some definitions specifically include religious motivations; others include hate, millenarian and apocalyptic groups. Several definitions refer only to non- state actors, whereas others include state-sponsored terrorism. Terrorism by groups is an essential part of several definitions, but some definitions include terrorism by individual actors[4].

The difficulty in defining terrorism is not new. Cooper, remarks that "there has never been since the topic began to command serious attention, some golden age in which terrorism was easy to define." Writing about terrorism in the middle of the 1970s, the political historian Walter Laquer threw up his hand; he viewed that providing a comprehensive definition was virtually impossible because of the great variety of circumstances in which this type of violence had appeared and the numerous and often competing political causes whose advocates had used it. Martha Crenshaw, another leading observer, wrote that the absence of a consensual definition continued to plague those interested in studying terrorism.[5]

Frequently what follows is a war of words, fought in a mass media, as each side denies that its behaviour constitutes terrorism as struggles to reach the moral high ground. More often, the mass media compound the confusion by applying the term 'terrorist' on a highly selective basis. Newspapers back and forth usually refer particular group as extremists, militants, guerrillas, 'terrorists' depending upon exceptionally hazy criteria.[6]

Hope springs eternal in the human breast, and perhaps for this reason alone, so many conferences and writings on the subject of terrorism begin with the obligatory, almost ritualistic recitation by the presenter of some preferred definition of terrorism. This is not wholly an exercise in futility; whatever the discrepancies detected by others, the definitions at least provide starting points for debate.[7] In a similar spirit, then, the following definitions of terrorism are offered here so that we may have a basis for reflection on the problems of terrorism.

Definitions Given by Academicians and Researchers

(1) According to Martha Crenshaw, - "Terrorism is a conspiratorial style of violence calculated to alter the attitudes and behaviour of multitude audiences. It targets the few in a way that claims the attention of the many. Terrorism is not a mass or collective violence but rather the direct activity of a small group."[8]

(2) Walter Laqueur in his book 'The Age of Terrorism' defined terrorism as - "Terrorism is the use or the threat of the use of violence, a method of combat, or a strategy to achieve targets. It aims to induce a state of fear in the victim, that is ruthless and does not conform with the humanitarian rules. Publicity is an essential factor in the essential factor in the terrorist strategy."[9]

(3) Bruce Hoffman, in his book ' Inside Terrorism' defined terrorism as "It is the deliberate creation and exploitation of fear through violence or threat of violence in the pursuit of political change."[10]

(4) Alex Schmid, Peter Jongman, defined terrorism as "An anxiety-inspiring method of repeated violent action, employed by (semi-) clandestine individual, group, or state actors, for idiosyncratic, criminal or political reasons....., whereby the direct target of violence are not the main targets. The immediate human victims of violence are generally chosen randomly (target of opportunity) or selectively (representative or

symbolic targets) from a target population, and serve as message generators."[11]

(5) According to Brian Jenkins "Terrorism is the use or threatened use of force designed to bring about political change."[12]

(6) James M. Poland defines terrorism as "It is the premeditated, deliberate, systematic murder, mayhem and threatening of the innocent to create fear and intimidation in order to gain a political or tactical advantage, usually to influence an audience."[13]

(7) Paul Wilkinson defines Terrorism as - "Coercive intimidation" which is in practice, "a systematic use of murder and destruction and the threat of murder and destruction in order to terrorise individuals, groups, communities or governments into conceding to the terrorists' political demand."[14]

Legal Definition of Terrorism

The laws relating to terrorism in democratic states too defines the term terrorism, which are as follows:-

(1) German Federal Republic: "Terrorism is the enduringly conducted struggle for political goals, which are intended to be achieved employing assaults on the life and property of other persons, especially through severe crimes detailed in Article 129 of the penal code."[15]

(2) United Kingdom: "For the Legislation, terrorism is the use of violence for political ends, and includes any use of violence to put the public or any section of the public in fear."[16]

(3) United States of America: "Premeditated, politically motivated violence perpetrated against noncombatant targets by sub-national groups or clandestine agents, usually intended to influence an audience."[17]

(4) The U.S. Department of Defense (DOD) has defined terrorism as "the calculated use of violence or threat of violence against individuals or property, to inculcate fear, intended to coerce or to intimidate government or societies in the pursuit of goals that are political, ideological or religious."[18]

(5) The Federal Bureau of Investigation defines terrorism as "The unlawful use of force or violence against persons or property to intimidate or coerce a government, the civilian population, or any segment thereof, in the furtherance of political or social objectives."[19]

(6) The Indian anti-terrorism law TADA 1987 defines terrorism as "The act done with the intent to overawe the Government as by law established or to strike terror in the people or any section of the people or to alienate any section of people or to adversely affect the harmony amongst different sections of the people, by using any of the lethal weapons mentioned in the Act in such a manner as to cause death of or injury to any person."[20] Another anti-terrorism law of India POTA 2002 also defines terrorism in the same manner as in TADA 1987.

International Organisations too tried to define the term terrorism; some of the definitions of terrorism which were framed under international legal regime are as follows:

(1) In 1937, the League of Nations drafted a definition of terrorism as "All criminal acts directed against a State and intended or calculated to create a state of terror in the minds of particular persons or a group of persons or the general public."[21]

(2) In 1992, a short legal definition proposed by terrorism expert, A.P. Schmid, to the United Nations Crime Branch, which defined terrorism as, "Act of terrorism = Peacetime equivalents to war crime."[22]

(3) In the year 1999, the General Assembly Resolution on Measures to Eliminate International Terrorism defined terrorism as "criminal acts intended or calculated to provoke a state of terror in the general public, a group of persons or particular persons for political purposes are in any circumstances unjustifiable, whatever the consideration of the political, ideological, racial, ethnic, religious or other nature that may be invoked to justify them."[23]

Consensus Definition of Terrorism

The two jurists, Brian Jeakins and Schmid, attempted to synthesise the consensus definitions. Brian Jenkin's after working for many years as a consultant on terrorism and counter-terrorism security and going through many definitions of terrorism proposed by many theorists and academicians, defined terrorism as, "terrorism is the use or the threatened use of force designed to bring about a political change."[24]

A.P. Schmid proposed small legal definition to the UN; further studied and reviewed many definitions, and he finds some twenty-two components that were common in one way or the other. He thereafter formulated a synthesised definition, which contained the common elements among twenty-two components of terrorism. According to Schmid: "Terrorism is an inspiring anxiety method of repeated violent action, employed by (Semi) clandestine individual, groups or state actors, for idiosyncratic, criminal or political reasons whereby-in contrast to assassination the direct target of violence are not the main targets. The immediate human victims of violence are generally chosen randomly (targets of opportunity) or selectively (representative or symbolic targets) from a target population, and serve as message generators. Threats and violence based communication processes between terrorist (organisation), (imperilled) victims, and main targets are used to manipulate the main target (audience), turning into a target of terror, a target of demands, or a target of attention, depending on whether intimidation, coercion, or propaganda is primarily sought."[25]

There is no established definition of terrorism. Academicians, researches, had given specific definitions, Democratic countries like U.S.A., India, U.K. too provided specific definitions of terrorism; and the world bodies like U.N. and other organisations were also working to chart out the definition of terrorism, but their efforts have failed in the face of widely divergent perceptions of what constitutes terrorism and who are terrorists. More than half-century have been wasted in trying to draft a comprehensive definition of terrorism, and at present also, we are not in a position to sit and discuss the best possible definition of terrorism. However, from the definitions mentioned above, we can, without any doubt, conclude that 'terror' is one of the essential elements of terrorism. Moreover, if any mission is accomplished through the employment of terrorist means, it will be a terrorist act, and this phenomenon will be termed as terrorism, no matter what is the purpose of the mission.

The definition of the term terrorism is embedded in a person's perspectives on terrorism. Perspective is a central consideration in defining terrorism. No matter how detached that observer is, it is hard to ignore the fact that the application of the term, calling some activity or group or organisation engaged in it "terrorist" conveys as moral judgment. They typically respond to an attempt at such labelling by denial and by making what amount to a counter-accusation. The government or organisation that made the initial claim is the 'real' terrorist by its commission of a litany of criminal or immoral acts and behaviour[26]. They adopt the mask of liberation, national ideality, religious fervour, and even democracy. Ethno nationalist and religious organisations such as Hamas (Islamic Resistance Movement) in Israel, Liberation Tigers of Tamil Eelam (LTTE) in Sri Lanka and the Provisional Irish Republican Army in the United Kingdom all declare that they are armies fighting on behalf of an oppressed people, and their supporters view them as freedom fighters.

On the other hand, many Israelis, Sinhalese and British would label members of these groups as terrorist.[27] The four perspectives that explain these critical situations are as follows: (1) Participants in a terrorist environment; (2) Terrorist or freedom fighter?; (3) Extremism or Mainstream?; and (4) Ideologies and Ideals.

Participants In A Terrorist Environment

People who participate in, or are affected by, terrorist incidents generally interpret the incident differently. They draw their conclusions regarding political violence without referring to the definitions of terrorism constructed by officials or experts. Usually, the participant in a terrorist environment consists of the following: The terrorist, the supporter, the victim, the target, the onlooker, and the analyst.

The perspective of the terrorist is that the violent incident is a justifiable act of war against an oppressive opponent. In so far as terrorist seek to attract attention, they target the enemy public or uncommitted bystanders. This is a legitimate tactic in their mind because, from their point of view, they are always freedom fighters and never terrorists.[28] Their perspectives are self-serving and just controversial as any academic or nation-states/government's attempt at defining terrorism. For example, the original Irish Republican Army

(IRA) elected to call itself an 'army' partly out of a desire to counter the label terrorist or the idea that their protest was in some way illegitimate. By calling themselves as 'army' and 'legal representative', the IRA becomes more like a government or a nation-state representative.[29] Supporters of terrorists are patrons, in essence, persons who provide a supportive environment or apparatus. Supporters will generally refer to the terrorist participants as freedom fighters. Even if supporters disagree with the use of force or with the application of force in a specific incident, they will often rationalise its use as the unfortunate consequence of a just war.[30]

Victims of political violence, and warfare, will rarely sympathise with the perpetrators of that violence, regardless of the underlying motive. From their perspective, the perpetrators are little better than terrorists. Targets are usually symbolic. They represent some feature of the enemy and can be either property targets or human targets. As is the case with the victim, human targets will rarely sympathise with the perpetrators. Onlookers are the broad audience to the terrorist incident. They can be directly affected by the incident at the scene of an attack or indirectly affected by modern mass media. The onlookers may either sympathise with the perpetrators or revile them or remain neutral. Depending on the world view of the onlooker, he or she might applaud a specific incident or a general dissident environment. The analyst is an interpreter of the terrorist incident. Analysts are essential participants because they create perspectives, interpret incidents, and label the other participants. Analysts can include political leaders, media experts and academic experts. Very often, the analyst will define for the other participant who is or is not a terrorist.[31]

Terrorism or Freedom Fighter

The second perspective is the determination of the question of whether the use of political violence is terrorism or freedom fighting. In general, those who resort to using the weapon of terrorism often consider themselves to be 'Freedom Fighter' struggling against oppression to establish a legitimate and desirable political objective.[32] They speak the language of liberation, national identity, religious fervour, and democracy. The terrorist organisations such as Hamas (Islamic Resistance Movement) in Israel, Liberation Tigers of Tamil

Eelam (LTTE) in Sri Lanka, and the Provisional Irish Republican Army (the Provos) in the United Kingdom label themselves as freedom fighters and their supporters too regards and respect them as freedom fighters fighting for the just cause.[33]

The declarations published by these and other organisations are in the language of liberation and freedom. For example, the leader of the LTTE delivered the following remarks on November 27, 2001, the LTTE's Hero's Day: "The Tamil people want to maintain their national identity and to live in their lands, in their historically given homeland with peace and dignity. They want to determine their political and economic life; they want to be on their own. These are the basic political aspirations of the Tamil people. It is neither separatism nor terrorism."

In the same way, the Palestinian Information Centre explained that: "Hamas is an acronym that stands for the Islamic Resistance Movement, a popular national resistance movement which is working to create conditions conducive to emancipating the Palestinian people, delivering them from tyranny, liberating their land from the occupying usurper, to stand up to the Zionist scheme which is supported by neocolonialist forces. Hamas is a part of Islamic awaking movement and upholds that this awakening is the road which will lead to the liberation of Palestine from the river to the sea. It is also a popular movement in the sense that it is a practical manifestation of a wide popular current that is deeply rooted in the ranks of the Palestinian people and the Islamic nation."[34]

It is often claimed, and without reason, that history is written by the winners, it is right in every aspect of life and stands right in the case of a victorious terrorist. A victorious terrorist becomes a statesman, and a failed terrorist remains a terrorist. Nelson Mandela and Menachem Begin were once regarded as a terrorist, but today they are respected as a statesman. Nelson Mandela was for a long time described as terrorist not only by the South African government but also by that of United States, as well as by many academics, though Mandela never, in fact, was qualified as a terrorist. Menachem Begin, however, is a different story. Begin led Irgun from 1943 until its dissolution in 1948. The Irgun was an illegal Jewish right-wing movement made up of Revisionist Zionists. They attacked both Arabs and British to establish a Jewish state on both sides of the river Jordan. In 1938 Irgun exploded land mines in an Arab fruit market in Haifa, killing seventy-four people. Most famously in 1946, they blew up the King David Hotel in Jerusalem, killing ninety-one people. Both Irgun and the Stern gang were absorbed into the fledgeling Israeli army on the expiration of the British mandate in 1948. Notwithstanding his past, Menacham Begin served as a Prime Minister of Israel from 1977 to 1983 and shared the prestigious Nobel Prize for peace with Anwar Sadat in 1978. In truth, Begin was a terrorist in the 1940s and a statesman in the 1970s.[35]

Those who were once labelled terrorists later become leaders of nations and heads of the states and terrorist organisations become the ruling parties. Taking into account such changes, other nations and the media accordingly revise their attitude towards them and further the difficulty in constructing the precise definition of terrorism. The saying "one man's terrorist is another man's freedom fighter", frustrates the process of definition, as it confuses the goal with the activity. If one likes the goals of the individual, she or he is a freedom fighter; if not, then she or he is a terrorist.

Extremism or Mainstreamism?

The third perspective is the determination of the question of whether political violence is a necessity or whether it is practised as a last resort. Members of the organisations such as Hamas, the LTTE, and the Provos admit that their methods are extreme, but they justify them as being proportional to the force used against them. Omar Sheik wrote in his confession that during his time as a student at the London School of Economics in 1992 'Bosina Week' was observed and several documentary movies were shown. He wrote that "one film, "The Death of a Nation", which depicted Serbs murdered Bosnian Muslims, shook my heart and launched his political and subsequent radicalisation. He helped to organise a student conference in Bosnia, and soon made contact with Islamic militants." Renato Curcio, the intellectual leader of the Italian left-wing social revolutionary group the Red Brigades, says that "he was converted to violence in reaction to an incident in which the police fired on farmworkers, killing two and injuring several children among many others." Vellupillai Prabhakaran, the poorly educated leader of the Sri Lankan nationalist group the Tamil Tigers, said: "It is the plight of the Tamil people that compelled me to take up arms. I felt outraged at the inhuman atrocities perpetrated against innocent people. The ruthless manner, in which our people were murdered, massacred, maimed …"[36]

Governments also adopted authoritarian measures to counter threats posed by these violent groups. As a result thereof, they (terrorist) rationalise their behaviour as a proportional response to an immediate threat. Number of cases of such rationalisation came into light, for example, when the Chilean and Argentine armed forces seized power during the 1970s and engaged in widespread violent repression of dissidents. In Argentina, nearly 30,000 people were said to have vanished during the so-called Dirty War waged by its military government from 1976 to 1983. Thus from the perspective of several violent organisations, extremist beliefs and terrorist methods are just and necessary and are considered to be a rational choice. They consider that no other method is better than violence in order to achieve freedom and to maintain order. On the other hand, those who oppose the practitioners of violence straightway reject their contentions and justifications of use of terrorist methods and perceive them as terrorists.[37]

Ideologies and Ideals

This perspective involves the ideologies and ideals that justify terrorist violence. Ideologies constitute political, social or economic beliefs. They guide the world view and manner of living for individuals, groups, and nations. They do not permit any deviations from their perceived truth and are completely intolerant of any criticism. The supporters and followers of particular ideology involve themselves in act violence and justify their actions by arguing that what they are doing is for the future betterment of the society in which they are living. Some ideological groups are Marxism, Anarchism, Fascism, and Nazism.[38]

The charismatic leader of the Tamil Tigers stated to an Indian reporter that he is waging war to make the life of Sri Lankan Tamilian better. He said after achieving its end the Tamil Eelam would be formed and this Tamil Eelam will be a socialist state, by socialism he meant an egalitarian society where human freedom and individual liberties will be guaranteed, where all forms of oppression and exploitation will be abolished. It will be a free society where our people will have the maximum opportunity to develop their economy and promote their culture. Tamil Eelam will be a neutral state, committed to non-alignment and friendly to India, respecting her regional policies, particularly the policy of making the Indian Ocean a zone of peace'.[39]

A member Ku Klux Klan, while delivering a speech to other members of the Klan group referred the death of four African American and compared them with animals. He stated "It was no shame they were killed. Why? Because when I go out to kill rattlesnakes, It does not make any difference between rattlesnakes and big snakes because I know it is like all snakes to be enemies and to poison me if they can. So, I kill them all, and if there are four less little niggers tonight, then I say, good for whoever planted the bomb. We are all better off."[40] The speaker here did not mention the word terrorist and justified the terrorist acts by comparing children to snakes, objects that can and have been killed by humans in self-defence.

Causes of Terrorism

Experts have long struggled to identify the central causes of terrorist violence. The most fundamental conclusion regarding the causes of terrorism is that there are some general causes besides particular ones because of the reason for the peculiar conditions, situations and cultural differences of different nations and countries. Terrorism is a tactic employed by many different groups in many different parts of the world in pursuit of many different objectives. It occurs in democracies, autocracies and most often, in transitional states. It would be nearly impossible to come up with a sole explanation for the behaviour and conduct of a Saudi cleric, a German university student, a Peruvian peasant, a Chechen soldier, a Japanese scientist and an Indian factory worker.[41]

There is no comprehensive theory to find out the reasons for terrorism. However, there are several different explanations which explain the causes of terrorism. The Psychological explanation states that the levels of the individual terrorist and the organisation all convey the knowledge of the causes of terrorism. The Sociological explanation argues that it is the socio-economic factors like poverty and inequality disclose causes. The Political explanation reveals that the cause of terrorism is the acts of the political will.

At the same time causes can be found in the religion and globalisation. Many of these causes are interwoven and interlinked and are quite challenging to separate. Terrorist fight for various reasons, some want a change in the political structure, like ethno-nationalist group; some want to bring about a revolution and introduce a new world order, like the social and revolutionary movements; some wants to roll back the clock to a halcyon era, like Islamic fundamentalists; and some like the Italian right-wing movements in Italy or the Protestants terrorist groups in Northern Ireland want to defend the status quo.[42]

Psychological Explanation

It is a common presumption that terrorists are mentally ill and psychopaths. It is said that terrorism is the outcome of insanity or mental illness, and terrorism is their trademark. However, the same is not valid, it has been found that their behaviour is neither insane nor irrational, and they are ordinary people. Experts state that the identity and desire to take revenge may be regarded as the leading cause of terrorism. They say that they (terrorists) engage themselves in such activities because of some significant incidents that occurred in their life, which influenced them significantly.[43]

Psychologist Eric D. Shaw through his "Personal Pathway Model" states why people indulge themselves in terrorist activities. The elements of this pathway model include early socialisation processes; narcissistic injuries; escalators events, particularly confrontation with police; and personal connections to the terrorist group members.

The Personal Pathway Model suggests that "terrorist came from a selected, at-risk population, who have suffered from early damage to their self-esteem. Their subsequent political activities may be consistent with the liberal social philosophies of their families but go beyond their perception of the contradiction in their family's beliefs and lack of their social action. Family political philosophies may also serve to sensitise these persons to the economic and political tensions inherent throughout modern society. As a group, they appear to have been unsuccessful in obtaining a desired traditional place in society, which has contributed to their frustration. The underlying need to belong to a terrorist group is symptomatic of an incomplete or fragmented psychosocial identity. Interestingly, the acts of security forces or police are cited as provoking more violent political activity by the individuals, and it is often a personnel connection to other terrorists which leads to membership in a violent group."[44]

The German militant Michael 'Bommi' Baumann, in his book 'How it all Began' writes that "it was the unprovoked killing by the German police of a student demonstrator against the shah of Iran that made him terrorist." Italian and German activists too held similar view to the Italian sociologist Donatella Della Porta. Members of the Finucane family described to the British reporter Kevin Toolis how they were enraged by the experience of being driven from their home by Protestant mobs. Moreover, Protestants' told BBC's Peter Taylor of being radicalised by the incidents of neighbours injured by IRA bombs.[45]

In several social and political contexts, political violence is a familiar social phenomenon for some people. When this process is combined with "the pronounced need to belong to a group", individuals can, in the end "define their social status by group acceptance."[46]The group provides a sense of belonging, a feeling of self-importance, and a new belief system that defines the terrorist act as morally acceptable and the group's goals as a paramount importance.[47] Shaw explains this as: "Apparently, membership in a terrorist membership in a terrorist group often provides a solution to the pressing personal needs of which the inability to achieve a desired niche in traditional society, albeit a negative one, which is commensurate with his or her prior expectations and sufficient to compensate for past losses. Group membership provides a sense of potency, an intense and close interpersonal environment, social status, potential access to wealth and a share in what may be a grand but noble social design. The powerful psychological forces of conversion in the group are sufficient to offset traditional social sanctions against violence. To the terrorist, their actions may have the moral status of religious warfare or political liberation."[48]

Social Explanation

The sociological explanation generally explains that terrorism is an outcome of deterioration of social values and intercommunity conflict and differences. This approach points out that terrorism can and does occur in both rich and emerging countries, but developing countries are more prone to it, and particularly those countries which are experiencing rocketing modernisation. In such countries, the process of socialisation of human culture and civilisation come into conflict, and as a result, thereof society becomes breeding ground of the evil of terrorism. Further, this approach states that the eventuality of terrorism is group-based and is considered as the weapons of the weak and these tactics are practised by them as a last resort. From the view of oppositionist, terrorism and other forms of collective violence are often described as 'senseless', and their participants are often depicted as irrational. However, the analysis does not fully stand complete, and it is because if 'rational' means goal-oriented...then most collective violence is indeed directed as achieving specific, social change-oriented goals, regardless of whether we agree with those goals or with violent means used to attain them. If 'rational' further means sound, wise, and logical, then available evidence indicates that collective violence is rational because it sometimes can help achieve their social goals.[49]

Changing economic condition results in instability, and the traditional thinking and practice of religion or local power, are challenged by the change. The nexus between poverty and terrorism has long been debated as a primary cause of terrorism, some experts ascribe to the impoverished refugee camps of the Middle East as the breeding ground for terrorists, and others point the relative affluence of many individual terrorists like Mohammad Atta, the mastermind of the 9/11 attacks, and more particularly to the wealth owned by Osama bin Laden. In-fact both the views are right, but if examined solely, then it fails to narrate the complete story.

Some academic investigations of the relationship between terrorism and poverty have asserted that they are, at best, indirect.[50] Among others, the most highly accepted explanation for the cause of terrorism is poverty and inequality, and it is argued that people adopt the practice of terrorism because of economic deprivation, but it is not entirely true. If there were a direct relationship between poverty inequality and terrorism, the developing nations having inequality in terms of wealth would have the highest rates of terrorism, but they do not. If there were a direct nexus between poverty and terrorism, then Africa, the poorest continent on the globe, would be facing the highest number of terrorist causalities, but it is not so. If terrorism is a consequence of inequality, states in Africa and Latin America with the maximum rates of inequality would have the highest rates of terrorism, but such is not the circumstances there.[51]In-fact many nationalist terrorist movements have been organised by ethnic groups who are quite well to do in terms of wealth, such as Tamils in Sri Lanka, the Sikhs in India, the Basques in Spain and the Catholics in Ireland.[52]

Though poverty and inequality may not be the cause of terrorism, it is inevitable that they are the risk factors that enhance the probability of terrorism. Further, once terrorism has commenced, poverty and inequality aggravates the chance that it will earn followers and supporters. Ted Robert Gurr in his academic work "Why Men Rebel", published in 1970 introduced the concept which was termed as 'Relative Deprivation Theory', according to this theory when a group's rising expectations are met by sustained repression or second class status, the group's reaction may include political violence. Their motive for engaging in politics is their observation that they are relatively deprived, in comparison to other groups, in an unfair social order. This should be distinguished with 'absolute deprivation' when a group has been deprived of the basic amenities which are necessary for survival by a government or social order. This state can also contribute to political violence. In other words, the force which drives the people to violence is not their absolute level of poverty but rather their position relative to others.[53]

Though the relative deprivation theory is very much popular among the experts, it is also not fully complete and has been criticised by some scholars. The psychological research suggests that aggression infrequently happens when the provisions for relative deprivation are met. This theory is more likely to explain individual behaviour rather than group behaviour and empirical studies have not found any relation between relative deprivation and political violence.[54]

Terrorism has occurred both in rich and poor countries, but developing countries are more prone to it. The rapid socio-economic changes are conducive to instability and inconstancy, which leads to erosion or deterioration of the traditional system of social control. These circumstances are then exposed to exploitation by militants offering to make sense of such changes, to blame others for the dislocations and humiliations involved, and to offer resources of redress. Only a small section of the population is required to be allured by the militants in order to bring to the evolution of a terrorist movement.[55] The glaring examples of the movements that are motivated against the government or social order include ethnic-nationalist movements such as Basque in Spain, Irish Catholics in Northern Ireland, Palestine in Israel, Sikhs in India, Tamils in Sri Lanka and French Canadians in Quebec.

Political Explanation

The political explanation explains that terrorism consists of strategic choices made by ideologically motivated revolutionaries who pursue victory by sheer force of will.[56]Terrorism is a tactic posited in political dissatisfaction, employed in the campaign of several diverse beliefs and doctrines that assist in legitimising and sustaining violence. Ideologies associated with nationalism, revolution, religion, and defence of the status quo have all inspired terrorism.[57]

In terms of revolutionaries' perspective, it is a rational decision to adopt a particular strategy and tactics to overcome their opponents. These strategies are the means of rational strategic choice wherein terrorism is adopted as a best-suited strategy. All that is necessary for assured needed victory is to possess the political and strategic will to achieve the ultimate goal. The exercise of terrorism as a strategic methodology is an execution evidenced on the experiences of every insurgent group so that its selection is the consequence or result of an evolutionary political progression.[58]Thus, "Perhaps because groups are low to recognise the extent of the limits to action, terrorism is often in a sequence of choices. It represents the outcome of a learning process. Experience in opposition provides radicals with information about the potential consequences of their choices. Terrorism is likely to be a reasonably informed choice among available alternatives, and some tried unsuccessfully."[59]

As a result thereof, terrorism is simply a means, an option or choice, selected by members of political fringe to achieve their ultimate end. Terrorism is a deliberate tactic, and from the point of view, success is ensured so long as the political group and their strategy remain strong.[60]

The Political approach, further state that natural stresses and strains of nation-building are the leading cause of terrorism. It argues, as countries go through the process of unification under a standard system of rules and institutions within the swathe of territory, they encounter resistance from within. New system of laws and institutions backed by a newly-constituted government will inevitably frighten some even as it reassures others. Classes, castes, religious and linguistic groups will all find themselves living under a new regime. The state has to enforce the new regime. In doing so, it may well alienate entrenched social and political interests who will then resist. Resistance may turn violent. If it does, the state will be constrained to restore law and order and will have to use violence, in turn, to do so. A cycle of violence and counter-violence will than ensue.[61]

Types of Terrorism

Terrorism has been classified by various academic experts such as:

(1) Barkan and Snowden has categorised terrorism as vigilante terrorism, insurgent, trans-national, and state terrorism;

(2) According to Hoffman, terrorism can be classified into ethno-nationalist/ separatist, international, religious, and state-sponsored terrorism.

(3) While undertaking the task of defining the New Terrorism, Laqueur contextualises far-rightist, religious state, "exotic", and criminal terrorism.

(4) Other academicians and researcher has classified terrorism into macro- terrorism, toxic terrorism, and net-war.

Terrorism broadly can be categorised into the following category after analysing all these classifications mentioned above:

(1) State Terrorism or Terrorism from above;

(2) Dissident Terrorism or Terrorism from Below;

(3) Religious Terrorism; and

(4) International Terrorism

State Terrorism or Terrorism from Above

'Terrorism from Above' means terrorism practised by the state directly or sponsored by state indirectly, by quasi-governmental agencies and personnel against perceived enemies.

Terrorism by states is characterised by official government support for policies of violence, repression, and intimidation. This violence and coercion are directed against perceived enemies that the state has determined to threaten its interests or security. Although the perpetrators of state terrorist campaigns are almost government personnel acting in obedience to directives originating from government officials, those who carry out the violence are also quite often unofficial agents who are used and encouraged by the governments.[62]

States that are inclined to use terrorism as an instrument of statecraft are often able to control the parameters for their involvement so that governments can sometimes manage how precisely a movement or an incident can be traced back to its personnel. The state sponsoring of terrorism is not always a straight forward process. It is usually a covert, secret policy that allows states to claim "deniability" when accused of sponsoring terrorism.[63]

States sponsors terrorism at two levels, one at the domestic level and the other at the international level. At the domestic level, state terrorism refers to the state's politically motivated application of force inside its borders. The state's military, law enforcement, and other security institutions are used to suppress perceived threats; these institutions can also be supplemented with assistance from unofficial paramilitaries and death squads. The purpose of domestically focused terrorism is to demonstrate the supreme power of the government and to intimidate or eliminate the opposition.[64]

State terrorism at an international level is practised by many governments as a policy option, as they cannot always deploy conventional armed forces to achieve their strategic objectives and goals. A report from Israel's International Policy Institute for Counter-Terrorism noted that "State-sponsored terrorism could achieve strategic ends where the use of conventional armed forces is not practical or useful. The high cost of modern warfare, and concern about non-conventional escalation, as well as the danger of defeat and the unwillingness to appear as the aggressor, have turned terrorism into an efficient, convenient, and generally discrete weapon for attaining state interests in the international realm."[65]

The practice of state terrorism at international domain is advantageous in several respects: (1) State terrorism is inexpensive; (2) State terrorism has limited consequences; and (3) State terrorism can be successful.

Dissident Terrorism or Terrorism from Below

The "Terrorism from Below" is committed by non-state movements; groups against governments, ethnonational groups, religious groups and other perceived enemies. It is practised by those outside the dominant group, usually focusing their violence and threats on those above. State repression and exploitation are the main reasons to explain why non-state actors resort to political violence. These grievances are often ignored by state officials, who refuse to act until they are forced to do so[66].Dissident terrorism may further be divided into:

(1) Communal Terrorism: Dissident terrorism is not always directed against a government or national symbols. It is often directed against entire population groups - people who are perceived to be ethnonational, racial, religious, or ideological enemies. Communal terrorism is "group against group" terrorism, whereby a subpopulation of society wags mutually destructive violence against each other. There are many sources of communal violence, such as ethno-nationalist, religious, and ideological.[67]

Ethno-nationalist communal terrorism involves conflict between populations that have distinct histories, customs, ethnic traits, religious traditions, or other cultural idiosyncrasies. In these conflicts, all sides believe themselves to be vulnerable and use this perception to rationalise engaging in terrorist violence.[68]

Religious communal terrorism refers to conflict between religious groups. It is sometimes one element of discord in a broader conflict between ethnonational groups. Many of the world's ethnic populations define their cultural identity partly through their religious beliefs so that violence committed by and against them has both ethnic and religious qualities. This linkage is standard in regions where ethnic groups with dissimilar religious beliefs have long histories of conflict, conquest, and resistance. In Sri Lanka, for example, the ongoing civil war between the Hindu Tamils and the Buddhist Sinhalese has been exceptionally violent, with massacres and indiscreet innate killings a common practice.[69]

Ideological communal terrorism reflected the global rivalry between the United States and the Soviet Union. The capitalist democratic West completed with the authoritarian communist East for influence in the postcolonial developing world in countries ravaged by invading armies during the war. A typical pattern was for civil wars to break out after European colonial powers or Axis armies were driven out of a country. These civil wars were fought by indigenous armed factions drawn from among the formerly occupied population. In China, Yugoslavia, Malaysia, and elsewhere, communist insurgents vied with traditional monarchists, nationalists, and democrats for power. Civilian casualties were high in all of these conflicts.[70]

(2) Religious Terrorism: Violence committed "in the name of the faith" has been a feature of human conflict since the early centuries of the previous millennium. Violence committed in the name of the faith is, from a religious perspective, desirable and pleasing to their God.[71] In the new era, it has become a binding ideology for many extremists, in part because it provides an uncomplicated sense of purpose and a clear world view.[72]

Religious terrorism is a type of political violence that is motivated by an absolute belief that an otherworldly power has sanctioned - and commanded - the application of terrorist violence for the greater glory of faith. Acts that are committed in the name of the faith will be forgiven by the otherworldly power and perhaps rewarded in an afterlife. In essence, one's religious faith legitimises violence so long as such violence is an expression of the will of one's deity.[73]

Religious terrorism is an idiosyncratic type of terrorism; it originates from countless rational, cultural, and historical contexts. As a basis for terrorism, religious faith has been applied in different ways, depending on the cultural and political environments of each terrorist movement.

"Holy Terror" was practised in earlier centuries by groups such as the Jewish Zealots, the Assassins, and the Thugs, and contemporary observers are particularly concerned about the growth of religious fanaticism. According to Laqueur, the new religious- terrorism is different from the old, aiming not a clearly defined political demands but at the destruction of society and the elimination of large sections of the population. In its most extreme form, this new terrorism intends to liquidate all of what it deems to be 'satanic forces,' which may exclude the majority of a country or humanity, as a precondition for the growth of another, better, and in any case different breeds of human. In its maddest, most extreme form it may aim at the destruction of all life on earth, as the ultimate punishment for humanity's crimes.' Some terrorists would like to impose their religion or political ideology on the whole world forcible captures this phenomenon when he notes that the "planet is falling precipitately apart and coming reluctantly together at the very moment." He labels this division as "Jihad" versus "McWorld".[74]

Religious terrorism can also be divided into state-sponsored religious terrorism and dissident religious terrorism. State-sponsored terrorism emanates from governments that pursue international agendas by mentoring and encouraging religious proxies. The glaring example of state-sponsored religious terrorism is Iranian support for Lebanon's Hezbollah. Dissident religious terrorism involves attacks by self-proclaimed "true believers" against members of other faiths and perceived apostasies within their faith.[75]

Classification of Terrorist Groups

The Institute for the Study of Conflict, U.S.A. had classified terrorist groups by dividing them into the following six main categories[76]:

(1) **Ethnic, Religious or Nationalist Groups:** These are minority groups who feel themselves to be different from the majority of the population on ethnic, religious, linguistic or cultural grounds. These may either right-wing or left-wing.

(2) **Extreme Leftist Groups:** These are several revolutionary groups of an extreme leftist ideology. They may often be at loggerheads with each other.

(3) **Anarchist Groups:** The anarchists are not necessarily the followers of the 19th-century revolutionary leader Bakunin but owe much to his ideas. They do not appear to have an exact theory about their final objectives. They are neither as numerous nor as relevant as the extreme leftist. The Angry Brigade in the United Kingdom could be counted in this category.

(4) **Pathological Groups or Individuals:** Where group violence appears to be a way of life in which the political objectives are never clearly spelt out. It may be convenient to regard such groups as pathological rather than political. The motivation may have more to do with personal inadequacy, hatred of family or specifically middle-class guilt feeling than with an acquired ideology.

(5) **Neo- Fascist and Extreme Right- Wing:** They may be less important as the extreme left in the current phase of history. Ordine Nero and Rosa Dei Venti of Italy could be classified in this category. The Neo-fascist and extreme right-wing groups sprung- up in reaction to the left-wing terrorism. Many times, they receive tactical support from the authorities.

(6) **Ideological Mercenaries:** Traditionally, mercenaries sell their military talents for money. The ideological mercenaries are ready to cross international borders in pursuit of ideological causes. For example, the terrorist organisation such as Al-Qaeda can be put under this group.

The Goals or Objective of Terrorists

Objectives and goals are theoretical concepts that help to explain the actions taken by extremist groups and movements during their struggle; they are a description of the process that moves toward outcomes.[77] The groups and individuals who carry out terrorist attacks have some broader goals, which are as follows:

Revolution

Before the collapse of the Soviet empire in 1989 and the subsequent disintegration of the Soviet Union itself in 1991, the world abounded with groups willing to use terrorism to bring about revolutionary social, economic and political change. Marx, Trotsky, Mao were typically their patron saints and Latin America was most often their venue. Argentina, Brazil, Uruguay, Colombia, and Peru had substantial "Urban guerilla" groups that seek to bring an end to the economic exploitation of workers and peasants and replace the prevailing political order with one more compatible with their socialist principles. Japan and the highly industrialised Western democracies also had a substantial number of like-minded organisations. The Italian Red Brigades, West Germany's Red Army Fraction, and the Japenese United Red Army may are some of the organisations which can be categorised having such an objective.[78]

Nationalism/Separatism

The objectives of terrorist groups, in this case, are national independence, the creation of independent states carved from territories that were previously under the control or part of some other country. For example, the Liberation Tigers of Tamil Eelam has carried out thousands of terrorist acts over more than two decades to establish an independent homeland for Sri Lanka's Tamil minority. Similarly, during the 1980s groups claiming to represent the Sikh population of India's Punjab state committed an extensive series of terrorist attacks, in order to create a separate state of Khalistan for Sikh population. The groups espousing nationalist/separatist causes usually display higher staying power than their revolutionary social parts.[79]

Religion

Since the Iranian Revolution of 1979 and the Soviet Union's military intervention in Afghanistan in the same year, groups claiming inspiration from religious ideas have come to play leading roles in terrorist activities around the world. Not religion in general but groups asserting their fidelity to Islam have become widely associated with particularly horrendous terrorist attacks, such as the September 11, 2001 attack by al-Qaeda on the World Trade Centre tower in New York City. Given the severity and volume of attacks carried out around the world by admirers or followers of Osama bin Laden the pre-occupation with Muslim fundamentalist or Islamist groups is perfectly understandable. The adherents of other religious traditions have been responsible for a significant number of terrorist attacks in recent years. In Israel followers of late Rabbi Meer Kahane were responsible for the execution of terrorist attacks or acts of "vigilante justice' against Palestinians on the West Bank. An Israeli zealot, the law student of Yigal Amir, invoked religious principles for his assassination of Prime Minister Yitzhak Rabin because of the latter's commitment of trading "land for peace" with the Palestinian Authority. In the United States followers of the Christian Identity movement, such as the Aryan Nations figures Robert Mathews and Buford Furrow, Jr. has carried out terrorist attacks against Jewish targets in order to carry out what they believe is the will of God by restoring the country to its rightful Aryan Christian people. In Japan members of the eclectic "new religion" Aum Shinrikyo (Supreme Truth), headed by the half-blind "prophet" Shoko Asahara, set off a canister of Sarin gas on a crowded Tokyo subway, killing twelve passengers and injuring many more.[80]

The religiously motivated terrorism appears to be more lethal because those who believe themselves to be acting on behalf of God and against the enemies of God feel less restrained in killing large numbers of people than terrorists driven by secular concerns.[81]

Single Issues

Whether religious or secular in outlook, most terrorist organisations claim to act on behalf of some broad political goal or set of goals. Campaigns of terrorist violence, though, have been carried out to achieve far more restricted aims. The legally protected ability of women to obtain abortions performed by licensed physicians in the United States has caused a backlash: a "right to life" movement has emerged, which is committed to ending this practice. On the movement's fringe single individuals (usually operating with networks of supporters) and small groups have assassinated doctors and nurses and bombed abortion clinics in order to make those seeking and performing abortions so fearful that they will desist from the practice. Also in the United States, the cause of environmental protection has led members of such groups as the Environmental Liberation Front (ELF) to fire-bomb expansion-minded ski resorts, construction sites and automobile dealership in order to deter further air pollution and the degradation of wildlife habitat.[82]

At last, however, it can be said that terrorism is a contextual phenomenon and the definitions, modes and ideologies of terrorism changes with the change in the society. What is necessary here is that we should treat this problem as not a common problem but should give proper attention. We should look into the causes of terrorism, and then systematically try to combat terrorism with an iron hand.

Notes

1. Joseph S. Tuman, *Communicating Terror: The Rhetoric Dimensions of Terrorism*, (2003), p. 2.
2. *Ibid.,* p. 3-4.
3. *Ibid.,* p. 4.
4. Pamala L. Griset, Sue Mahan (ed.), *Terrorism in Perspective*, (2003), p. xii.
5. Leonard Weingberg, *Global Terrorism, A Beginner's Guide*, (2006), p. 1.
6. *Ibid.,* p. 2.
7. *Ibid.*
8. Joseph S. Tuman, *Communicating Terror: The Rhetoric Dimensions of Terrorism*, (2003), p. 5.
9. *Ibid.*
10. Leonard Weingberg, *Global Terrorism: A Beginner's Guide*, (2006), p. 3.
11. *Ibid.*
12. R.P.Kataria and S.K.A Naqvi, *Laws on Prevention of Terrorism and Unlawful Activities alongwith International Terrorism,* (2003), p. 108.
13. Shamsida Tayab, "Human Approach and Tolerance sans POTO and Majoritarian Tryanny: The need is action and not the reaction against terrorism in India", Dr. S.A.K. Azad (ed.) *Laws on Prevention of Terrorism*, (2003), p. 48.
14. EdgarO Balance, *Terrorism in the 1980s*, (1989), p. 16.

15. Leonard Weingberg, *Global Terrorism: A Beginner's Guide*, (2006), p. 3.
16. *Ibid.*
17. *Ibid.,* p. 4.
18. Joseph S. Tuman, *Communicating Terror: The Rhetoric Dimensions of Terrorism*, (2003), p. 7.
19. *Ibid.*
20. Section 3 of the TADA 1987.
21. Joseph S. Tuman, *Communicating Terror: The Rhetoric Dimensions of Terrorism*, (2003), p. 7.
22. *Ibid.*
23. *Ibid,* p. 11.
24. *Ibid,* p. 8.
25. Joseph S. Tuman, *Communicating Terror: The Rhetoric Dimensions of Terrorism*, (2003), p. 14.
26. Leonard Weingberg, *Global Terrorism: A Beginner's Guide*, (2006), p. 3.
27. Gus Martin, *Understanding Terrorism: Challenges Perspective and issues*, (2006), p. 53.
28. *Ibid.,* p. 51.
29. Joseph S. Tuman, *Communicating Terror: The Rhetoric Dimensions of Terrorism*, (2003), p. 9.
30. Gus Martin, *Understanding Terrorism: Challenges Perspective and issues*, (2006), p. 51.
31. *Ibid,* p. 51-52.
32. Edgar O' Balance, *Terrorism in the 1980s*, (1989), p. 10.
33. Gus Martin, *Understanding Terrorism: Challenges Perspective and issues*, (2006), p. 53.
34. Palestinian Information Centre. Hamas website, www.Palestine-info.com, accessed on 30/11/2005.
35. Louise Richardson, *What Terrorists Want: Understanding The Terrorist Threat*, (2006), p. 27-28.
36. *Ibid.,* p. 62-63.
37. Gus Martin, *Understanding Terrorism: Challenges Perspective and issues*, (2006), p. 54.
38. *Ibid,* p. 55.
39. Louise Richardson, *What Terrorists Want: Understanding Terrorist Threat*, (2006), p. 112.
40. Joseph S. Tuman, *Communicating Terror: The Rhetoric Dimensions of Terrorism*, (2003), p. 10.
41. Louise Richardson, *What Terrorists Want: Understanding Terrorist Threat*, (2006), p. 60.
42. *Ibid,* p. 60-61.
43. Gus Martin, *Understanding Terrorism: Challenges Perspective and issues*, (2006), p. 96.

44. Rex A. Hudson, *The Sociology and Psychology of Terrorism: Who Becomes a Terrorist and Why?*, A Report Prepared under an Interagency Agreement by the Federal Research Division, Library of Congress, September 1999, p. 25, at http://www.loc.gov/rr/frd/. Accessed on 24 April 2006.
45. Louise Richardson, *What Terrorists Want: Understanding Terrorist Threat*, (2006), p. 62.
46. Gus Martin, *Understanding Terrorism: Challenges Perspective and issues*, (2006), p. 96.
47. Rex A. Hudson, "The Sociology and Psychology of Terrorism: Who Becomes a Terrorist and Why?", *A Report Prepared under an Interagency Agreement by the Federal Research Division, Library of Congress*, September 1999, p. 34, at http://www.loc.gov/rr/frd/. Accessed on 24 April 2006.
48. *Ibid.* p. 34-35.
49. Barkan, Steven E., and Lynne L. Snowden, *Collective Violence*, (2001), p. 6.
50. Alan Krueger and Jitka Maleckova, NBER Working Paper no. w9074, Cambridge, MA: National Economic Research, 2002. See also Krueger and Maleckova, 'Does Poverty cause Terrorism? *New Republic*, June 24, 2004.
51. *Human Development Report 2005*, Chapter 2: Inequality and Human Development (New York;' United Nations Development Programme), http://undp.org/report/global/2005. Accessed on January 5 , 2006.
52. Louise Richardson, *What Terrorists Want: Understanding Terrorist Threat*, (2006), p.78.
53. Barkan, Steven. E, and Lynne L. Snowden, *Collective Violence*, (2001), p. 18. See Davies, James Chowning, "Towards a Theory of Revolution". *American Sociological Review* 25 (1962): 5-19. Also see Ted Robert Gurr, *Why Men Rebel*, Princeton University Press (1972).
54. Barkan, Steven E., and Lynne L. Snowden, *Collective Violence*, (2001), p. 17.
55. Louise Richardson, *What Terrorists Want: Understanding Terrorist Threat*, (2006), p. 82.
56. See Crenshaw, Martha, "The Logic of Terrorism: Terrorist Behaviour as a Product of Strategic Choice". Reich Walter, (ed.) *Origin of Terrorism: Psychologies, Ideologies, Theologies, State of Mind,* Woodrow Wilson Centre, (1998), p. 7-24.
57. See Crenshaw, Martha, "Political Explanation", *In Addressing the Causes of Terrorism- The club de Madrid Series on Democracies and Terrorism, vol. I. The International Submit on Democracy, Terrorism and Security.* (8-11 March 2005 Madrid).
58. Martin, Gus, *Understanding Terrorism: Challenges Perspective and issues*, (2006), p. 90.
59. See Crenshaw, Martha, "*The Logic of Terrorism: Terrorist Behaviour as a Product of Strategic Choice*". Reich Walter, (ed.) *Origin of Terrorism: Psychologies, Ideologies, Theologies, State of Mind*, Woodrow Wilson Centre, (1998), p. 7-24.
60. Martin, Gus, Understanding *Terrorism: Challenges Perspective and issues*, (2006), p. 90.
61. Kanti P. Bajpai, *Roots of Terrorism*, (2002), p. 26.

62. Gus Martin, *Understanding Terrorism: Challenges Perspective and Issues*, (2006), p. 111-112.
63. *Ibid.*
64. *Ibid.*, p. 131.
65. International Policy Institute for Counter-Terrorism, Herliya, www.ict.org.il/interter/org.cfm. Accessed on 25/1/2007.
66. Gus Martin, *Understanding Terrorism: Challenges Perspective and Issues*, (2006), p. 131.
67. *Ibid.*, p. 171.
68. *Ibid.*
69. *Ibid.*
70. *Ibid.*, p. 171.
71. *Ibid*, p. 175.
72. Charles Krauthammer, 'The Unipolar Moment Revisited', Gus Martin(ed.) *The New Era of Terrorism: Selected Readings*, (2004), p. 14.
73. Gus Martin, *Understanding Terrorism: Challenges Perspective and issues*, (2006), p. 184.
74. Margaret Atwood, 'International Terrorism', Pamala L. Greiset and Sue Mahan (eds) *Terrorism in Perspective*, (2003), p. 49.
75. Gus Martin, *Understanding Terrorism: Challenges Perspective and Issues*, (2006), p. 214.
76. Dweep Chand Singh, 'Causes and Psychological Management of Terrorism', M.G.Hussain(ed.) *Terror, Torture and Terrorism: Facets of Human Behaviour*, (2006), p. 161.
77. Gus Martin, *Understanding Terrorism: Challenges Perspective and issues*, (2006), p. 272.
78. Leonard Weingberg, *Global Terrorism: A Beginner's Guide*, (2006), p. 8.
79. *Ibid.*
80. Sean K. Anderson and Stephen Sloan, *Historical Dictionary of Terrorism*, (2002), p. 9.
81. *Ibid.*
82. *Ibid.*, p. 9.

Chapter - 2

Terror Laws in India and Rule of Law

Introduction

The world is passing through difficult days. Number of problems are surfacing from time to time. One such problem faced by the world including India is the menace of terrorism. Terrorism has become the order of the day. It has engulfed entire world, every section of people and poses extraordinary challegnges to the civilised world. India, got freedom from the British Raj in the year 1947, but problems such as poverty, unemployment, illiteracy, health and medical problems, economic disparity, social exploitation etc. dominated the independent India.

Initially, the menace of terrorism was not so aggravated in nature and was considered to be the ordinary problem concerning law and order. However, in due time, it spread its tentacles in every nook and corner of the country. The devasating nature of terrorism in India compelled the government to legislate specific anti-terror laws to counter the menace of terrorism.

Terrorism in India

India is with war of terror, and since 1947 is experiencing terrorism and destructive activities sponsored by Pakistan and China. Initially, Indian faced Pakistan's sponsored terrorism in Jammu and Kashmir and, later, China sponsored such activities in the north-east. At international level such terror activities in India was recognised as as insurgency movements and proxy wars or low-intensity conflicts, and not as State sponsored terrorism.[1]

The problem of terrorism in India is different from the problem of terrorism faced by other countries. As various types of terrorism is rooted in India, such as religious, ethnic, ideological, secessionist and externally motivated. Thus the root causes of terrorism spread over to different parts of India is different and therefore the position of India in relation with terrorism is very complex.[2]

India is/was facing the Khalistan oriented terrorism in Punjab based on a dream of a "theocratic state through secession[3]; Militants terrorism sponsored by Pakistan in Jammu and Kashmir[4]; The Naxalite movement which took shape of terrorism in Bengal, Bihar, Andhra Pradesh, Chattisgarh and Jharkhand is based on "identity crisis"[5]; The ULFA terrorism in Assam[6]; The Nagaland and Mizo terrorism is based on "identity crisis"[7]; and The Manipur and Tripura terrorism based on the "grievance situation."[8]

Laws Concerning Terrorism in India

Terror activities cannot provide freedom or justice. Hence, such activites cannot be termed as the struggle to achieve equality, liberty and justice. On the contrary, terrorism is a threat to equality, liberty and justice.[9] The darkest truth is that terrorists perpetuated horrifying barbarity and the Indian government was not able to tackle the acts of terrorism. The government lacked the manupultaive tactics to internationalise such menace in comparison to United States and Israel. However, in response to the menace of terrorism the Indian government enacted anti-terrorism laws, from time to time.

In 1980s India evidenced a sharp increase in terrorist activities. Thus, the government was compelled to legislate the first the anti-terrorism law The Terrorists and Disruptive Activities (Prevention) Act 1985 (TADA). This Act was initially enacted for the duration of two years. However, the menace of terrorism intensified and thus the life of TADA was extended from time to time. However, TADA was opposed by civil societies, human rights activicts, lawyers and even National Human Rights Commission (NHRC) recommened to repeal the TADA as its provisions were misused in a number of cases. Finally the life of TADA was expired in the year 1995.

TADA was intended to be used in the terrorism affected area, however, it was evidenced that this was more implemented in the states least affected with terrorism. According to the available sources, the person charged under TADA were in between thirty to sixty per cent were residents of such states which were least affected by terror activities.[10] Several innocent people were arrested under TADA not only from the Punjab and the State of Jammu and Kashmir but also from other states. People from all section of society, which included, political activists, leaders of Kisan movements, trade union leaders, students, lawyers, journalists and even creative writers were arrested under TADA.[11] The State of Punjab and The State of Jammu and Kashmir were the worst affected states by terrorism, however, it was the State of Gujarat where maximum number of people were arrested under TADA.[12] As per the Government statistical information by May 1993 the total number of person detained under TADA was 52998. The number of person detained under TADA in Gujarat was 17000 nearly thirt two percent of the total. However, in the State of Jammu and Kashmir, only 1826 person were detained under the same law, in Andhra Pradesh the number was 5614 nearly 10.74% in the same period. In Punjab 7969 (41.32%) had been detained under TADA till September 1989 out of 19286 in the country, 9552 (36.3%) persons out of 26261 in March 1990, 12180 (31.16%) persons out of 39089 in March 1991, and 14458 (27.66%) persons out of 52268 in February 1993.[13]

According to the Ministry of State for Home Affairs out of 67,059 persons were detained under the said Act since the enactment of the Act, however, only 8,000 were tried and only 725 accused were convicted. The most striking example of terrorists ducking TADA was operation Black Thunder in Assam. All forty-six persons charged under TADA were discharged due to the technicality. On the one hand, the arrest under TADA was mounting at frenetic rate on the other hand the conviction rate was falling which buttressed the distrust of the human rights advocates and civil socities that this Act was utilised more as an instrument to enable preventive detention and police abuse than as a meaningful and effective criminal law to combat terrorism.[14]

Since the misapplication and abuse of TADA had become the norm, momentum in favour of its repeal began to build up, as the supposed benefits according from it were overweighed by the instances of misuse. The question raised was: Has TADA performed a perceptibly useful function in combating terrorism? Answering this question, the senior police officers in Punjab, Kashmir, Maharastra and Delhi were positive in replaying this question, they said that TADA is the most useful legislation to tackle the problem of terrorism, Prakash Singh DGP even went on saying that said that repealing TADA would be like "Throwing the baby out with the bath water". But, on the other hand, a large section people who contented those realities on the ground indicated that TADA incrementally added little to the anti-insurgency or terrorist operations.

The National Human Rights Commission (NHRC) in the year 1994 adopted a unique strategy to address the issues that surfaced due to the TADA. firstly, it monitored the application of TADA provisions by State machinery. Secondly, prepared a dossier to satisfy the Supreme Court to recondier its decision as given in Kartar Singh *v* Union of India. And lastly, the NHRC started convincing the member of Parliament not to renew TADA.[15] In February 1995, the then Chair Person of NHRC, Justice Ranganath Misra, wrote a letter to all members of Parliament urging them not to renew TADA. When TADA came up for renewal, the congress-led government did not try to extend the period of the said Act but allowed to expire on May 23, 1995.[16]

However, the TADA was repealed but menace of terrorism prevailed. Thus, to counter Terrorism, the Law Commission of India was assigned the task of drafting a new statute and the Criminal Law Amendment Bill 1998. Nevertheless, both the Bills met with strong opposition. Further, the Government introduced the Prevention of Terrorism Bill, 2000 considering the recommendations given by the Law Commission of India.[17]It was recommended by the Law Commission that to fight the menace of terrorism effectively and effieicntly a legislation is *sine quo non* which provides some extraordinary powers to State machinery.[18] According to the Law Commission: "Given the prevailing situation in the country…, the Law Commission of India agrees with the opinion of the Government of India that India too requires a permanent anti-terrorist law. Over the past few years, the security situation both within and around the country has indeed worsened, and international terrorism is assuming proportions. As already stated, India has become one of the prime targets of both international and domestic terrorism, which has in its command - enormous funds, arms, modern communication equipment and contacts. The threat is serious and has to be fought with determination."[19]

The Law Commission based its recommendations on the premise that the security of India is at stake, as the government is fighting this menace with iron hand. The Indian government had gone too soft. This soft state argument was the heart of the 'working paper' on terrorism. The Commission viewed that: "A perception has developed among the terrorist groups that the Indian State is inherently incapable of meeting their challenge, that it has become soft and indolent. Quite a few parties have developed a vested interest in a soft state, a weak government and ineffective implementation of the laws. Foreign funds are flowing substantially to various organisations and groups which serve, willingly or unwillingly, the long term objectives of a foreign power."[20]

It was further stated by the Commission further that: "An extraordinary situation calls for an extraordinary law, designed to meet and check such extraordinary situations. It is one thing to say that we must create and provide internal structures and safeguards against possible use and abuse of the Act and altogether a different thing to say that because a law is liable to be misused, we should not have an Act at all."[21]

Thus, the Law Commission's main reason for enactment of anti-terrorism law was three-pronged. First, that the terrorism is increased in its very nature and hence the security of India is threatened; secondly, because India is soft on terrorists; and thirdly, apprehension of abuse of anti-terrorism laws did not build up a strong ground to reject such laws altogether.[22] However, The debate on the need of a stricter law to combat terrorism generated in the wake of the proposal to enact the Prevention of Terrorism Bill, 2000 into the law based on the 173rd Report of the Law Commission of India impelled the National Human Rights Commission to give its opinion on the subject.

Giving its opinion on the Prevention of Terrorism Bill, 2000 the NHRC referred to the existing laws on the subject and emphasized that the real deficiency was in their implementation and not the content.[23] NHRC concluded that: "...and consistent with the view that it took in respect of TADA, the commission is now unanimously of the considered view that there is no need to enact a law based on the Draft of Prevention of Terrorism Bill, 2000 and the needed solution can be found under the existing laws, if properly enforced and implemented, and amended, if necessary. The proposed Bill, if enacted, would have the ill-effect of providing unintentionally a strong weapon, capable of gross misuse and violation of human rights which must be avoided particularly in view of the experience of the misuse in the recent past of TADA and earlier of MISA of emergency days. This commission regrets its inability to agree with the opinion of the Law Commission in its 173rd Report and recommends that a new law based on the Draft of Prevention of Terrorism Bill, 2000 be not enacted."[24]

Utilising the international situation after September 11, 2001 (World Trade Centre, New York attack) and the perception of a national security threat created by the attack on the Indian Parliament on 13th December 2001, the Government called an extraordinary joint session of Parliament, as this was the only way to muster the majority required to pass the Bill.[25] It was only the third time in the history of the Indian Parliament that the extraordinary measure of calling a joint session was taken. On 26th March 2002, hastily, POTA become law.[26]

Considerable apprehensions about the misuse of POTA was from the civil socities, human rights activists as well as from common people. Such apprehension was primarily based on the experience with TADA and on the contents of the law itself. Moreover, Justice Krishna Iyer, the eminent judge and commentator, cautioned that in the guise of anti-terrorist enactment, everything precious in our constitution sanctified criminal justice could not be subverted.[27] Further, the People Union for Democratic Rights (PUDR) vehemently argued, against enacting POTA and observed that: "The premise of such a demand is that the ordinary law and normal criminal justice system have failed to cope with these crimes. The failure is not attributed to the law enforcing machinery—its inefficiency or corruption—but to a weakness of law based on principles of liberal jurisprudence and notions of natural justice, principles like the right to equal treatment before the law, the right to fair trial and the right to be deemed innocent until proven guilty beyond reasonable doubt. Thus, if the law is to be effective in dealing with terrorists, it can only do so if these principles are overturned and these rights are taken away."

However, the brief history of the POTA demonstrated that like TADA, it was also misused and applied innocent people and the apprehension of misuse of POTA was not belied. For example, in Jharkhand, where the highest numbers of POTA cases and detenues were registered, the protesting tribal community had been targeted. In Gujarat, all except one of the POTA detainees were from the Muslim minority, in Tamil Nadu, political opponents were booked, and in Uttar Pradesh, the so-called anti-terror law has been used against poor communities.[28] The vehement criticisation of POTA from every corner of the country compelled the government to repeal POTA.

Subsequently, after the repeal of POTA, the Unlawful Activities Prevention Act, 1967 (UAPA) was amended in the year 2004, and several provisions of POTA were enshrined in it. Consequently, UAPA was amended several times and making it more harsher and stricter than TADA and POTA. The amendment in the year 2019 in UAPA enshrined provisions which are against the well established principle of human rights. The Amendment Act of 2019 confers the power on Central Government to designate even an individual as a terrorist. It can be said that UAPA is nothing but a new avatar of earlier anti-terror law of India. By amending UAPA and making it harsher and stricter the government is doing nothing but pouring old wine in new bottle. Moreoever, the difference between the Indian anti-terror laws with that of US and UK anti-terror laws is that the later countries laws are against the aliens or non-citizens, on the other hand the Indian laws are applied to its own citizens.[29]

The anti-terrorism laws in India overturn every tenet of democracy, violates the fundamental rights enshrined in the Constitution, and violates every provision in the criminal justice system, which is meant to safeguard the innocent people. It seems that Indian Government enacted draconian laws were basically to justify repression of domestic dissent and political opposition which lead to unwarranted infringement of civil rights, as the measures provided in the Act erodes core human rights safeguard. Non-violent activities have been considered as terrorism, and excessive measures have been adopted to restrict individual rights including the presumption of innocence, the right to a fair trial, freedom from torture, privacy rights, freedom of expression, freedom of press and assembly and the right to seek asylum.

Constitutional Validity of Anti-terror Law

The constitutional validity of TADA was examined by Supreme Court after a long period of its existence in the case of Kartar Singh v State of Punjab. The validity or legality of the said Act was chiefly challenged on the following grounds: (1) that the central legislature has no competence to enact this legislation; (2) that the said Act and many of the provisions enshrined under the Act is clearly in violation of Fundamental Rights in Part III of the Indian Constitution. It was also asserted that the Act absolutely ignored and violated the humanitarian law and universal human rights. The provisions of the Act were not in tune with the basic test of justice and fairness which are well recognized principles of law. The petitioners projected the Act as draconian, ugly, vicious, harsh, oppressive and highly repressive.

The Apex Court upheld the constitutional validity of the Act as a whole and various provisions which were challenged except section 22 of the Act which was declared unconstitutional and struck down. Though the constitutional validity of the TADA was upheld by the Supreme Court, the Court laid stress on checks and balances on its use. The Court also observed that a delicate checks and balance needs to be drawn to protect the innocent from conviction and the need of the society to ensure that the offender is punished.

In Kartar Singh v State of Punjab[30], the Apex Court observed: "It is true that on many occasions, we have come across cases wherein the prosecution unjustifiably invokes the provisions of the TADA Act with an oblique motive of depriving the accused persons from getting bail and in some occasions when the courts are inclined to grant bail in cases of registered under ordinary criminal law, the investigating officers in order to circumvent the authority of the courts invoke the provisions of the TADA Act. This kind of invocation of the provisions of TADA in cases, the facts of which do not warrant, is nothing but sheer misuse and abuse of the Act by the police."

The Court further stated that: "We are undoubtedly committed to uphold human rights even as a part of long standing heritage and as enshrined in our constitutional law. We feel that this perspective needs to be kept in view by every law enforcing authority because the recognition of inherent dignity and of the equal and inalienable rights of the citizens is the foundation of freedom, just and peace in the world. If the human rights are outrage, then the court should set its face against such violation of human rights by exercising its majestic judicial authority."[31]

The constitutional validity of POTA is challenged in case of Simranjit Singh Mann *v* Union of India[32], and before Supreme Court of India in case of P.U.C.L and Anr. *v* Union of India[33]. The Supreme Court and the Punjab High Court observed that: "Fight against the overt and covert acts of terrorism is not a regular criminal justice-endeavour. Rather it is defence of our nation and its citizens. It is a challenge to the whole nation. The Government is charged with the duty of protecting the unity, integrity, secularism and sovereignty in India from terrorists, both from outside and within borders. In the above circumstances Parliament felt that a new anti-terrorism law is necessary for a better future."

The court further observed that : "The terrorist threat that we are facing today is now on an unprecedented global scale. Terrorism has become a global threat with global effects. It has become a challenge to whole community of civilized nations. Many happenings in the recent past caused the international community to focus on the issue of terrorism with renewed intensity. The Security Council unanimously passed resolutions 1368 (201) and 1373 (2001); the General Assembly adopted resolution 56/1 by consensus, and declarations inter-alia calls upon member states to take, necessary steps to 'prevent and suppress terrorist acts' and also to prevent and suppress the financing of terrorist acts.' India is a party to all these resolves. It has thus become our international obligation also to enact necessary laws to fight terrorism." "Parliament has passed POTA by taking all these aspects into account. To meet such a situation, a law can be enacted only by Parliament and not by state legislature…Parliament has explored the possibility of employing the existing laws to tackle terrorism and arrived at the conclusion that the existing laws are not capable. It is also clear to Parliament that terrorism is not a usual law and order problem. The Court further observed that mere possibility of abuse cannot be counted as a ground for denying the vesting powers or declaring a statute unconstitutional."

However, while upholding the constitutional validity of the POTA, the observed that, "The protection and promotion of human rights under the rule of law is essential in the prevention of terrorism. Here comes the role of law and court's responsibility. If human rights are violated in the process of combating terrorism, it will be self-defeating. Terrorism often thrives where human rights are violated, which adds to the need to strengthen action to combat violations of human rights. The lack of hope for justice provides breeding grounds for terrorism. Terrorism itself should also be understood as an assault on basic rights. In all cases, the fight against terrorism must be respectful to the human rights."

After the Mumbai Terror attack in the year 2008, the Indian Government enacted a federal law, National Investigation Agency Act to combat terrorism. The constitutionality of this Act was also challenged before the Mumbai High Court in the case of Pragyasingh Thakur *v* State of Maharashtra.[34] It was contended that the Parliament lacks competency to constitute an agency for the investigation of offences as the policing stands in the State List of the Seventh Schedule to the Constitution. The Court rejected the contention by noting the entries in List-I and in List-III and by reading them together and harmoniously came to the conclusion that the Parliament is competent to enact the NIA Act. The Court, further stated that when the parliament is competent to enact the law for the subjects enumerated in the schedule to the NIA Act, it is equally competent to create an agency for the investigation of the offences specified in it.

The Court further observed that "If the investigating agencies are set up, but there is no prohibition against the investigations being carried out or handed over to any agency other than a named agency, then, we do not see how by mere change or shifting of the agency the Parliament can be seen as encroaching upon the powers of the State Legislature. Even in matters confined to the State the investigations can be handed over or taken over by a Central Investigation Agency like CBI and in exceptional circumstances. If that does not violate or contravene the constitutional provisions and particularly dealing with distribution of legislative powers, then, all the more the NIA Act cannot be declared as unconstitutional. In other words, by a wholistic approach and harmonious reading of the constitutional provisions and entries in the schedule, it will be permissible to hold that the Parliament was competent to enact the NIA Act, 2008."

However, the application of NIA is also tainted. The surprising facts revealed by the Special Public Prosecutor, that she was directed not to plead the strongly in a case related to terror attack on Malegaon.[35] In another case, in which persons associated with RSS were accused (Ajmir Dargah Bomb Blast Case), the Public Prosector was disappointed with NIA's lack of interest during trial of the case. Yet in other cases such as Samjhauta Express bomb blast case and Hyderabad Mecca Masjid Blast Case the conduct of NIA is looked in suspicion.[36]

Anti-terrorism Law vis a vis Rule of Law

The act of terror is the real threat to the integrity and security of the country, and it is the primary responsibility of the state in a democratic rule to provide security, freedom and liberty to the people. Thus, the government is empowered to enact anti-terror laws to curb the menace of terrorism. However, the state should take precaution while enacting such laws, so that the rights of the innocent people are not offended as laws derive strength not only from the authority of the State but also from the support of the people. Moti Lal Nehru, while addressing Amritsar Congress Session in 1919 (though in reference of Rowlatt Act) observations very well fit in case of anti-terrorism laws. He stated that: "No one can but deplore violence and political crime. But let us not forget that it is the outcome of continued repression. It is due to the perversity of the executive which blinds itself to the causes of the discontent and like a mad bull, goes about attacking all who dare stand up against it."[37]

Democratic correction is not merely in-laws; it is much more in the vibrant functioning of the administrative and political institutions. Inequality before the law or economic, social-political, cultural factors and even uneven application of the law must come to an end as these factors fuel the terrorism. National Human Rights Commission observed that: "...the war against terrorism must be fought boldly and won. But this duty, for all of the difficulties it entails, must be accomplished in a manner that accords with an uncompromising adherence to the provisions of the Constitution of the Republic, the laws of our land, and relevant international instruments, including those of human rights, to which India is a state party."[38]

The apex court in case of Niranjan Singh Karan Singh Punjabi *v.* Jitendra Bhimraj[39] observed: "When a law visits a person with serious penal consequences, extra care must be taken to ensure that those whom the legislature did not intend to be covered by the express language of the statute are not roped in by stretching the language of the law." Security of the society is unquestionably the vital aim of the welfare state, but it is not the sole aim of the state. One of the most significant and foremost duties of the state is to protect the fundamental rights guaranteed in the Constitution. It would be ironic if in the name of combating terrorism, the rule of law is kept aside and the state violates the rights of the citizens.

Democracy is the antithesis of terrorist tyranny, which is why the terrorists denounce it and are willing to kill the innocent to stop it. Democracy is based on empowerment, while the terrorists' ideology is based on enslavement. Democracies expand the freedom of their citizens, while the terrorists seek to impose a single set of narrow beliefs. Democracy sees individual as equal in worth and dignity, having an inherent potential to create, governs them, and exercise basic freedoms of speech and conscience. The terrorists see individual as objects to be exploited, and then to be ruled and oppressed.[40] Moreover, if in combating terrorism the nations violate the basic norms of democracy and human rights then it will be a win-win situation for terrorists as they have the main goal to demolish the democratic structure of the world order and create chaos. The apex court in case of People's Union for Civil Liberties *v* Union of India[41] observed that: "The protection and promotion of human rights under the rule of law is essential in the prevention of terrorism. Here comes the role of law and the court's responsibility. If human rights are violated in the process of combating terrorism, it will be self-defeating. Terrorism often thrives where human rights are violated, which adds to the need to strengthen action to combat violations of human rights. The lack of hope for justice provides breeding grounds for terrorism. Terrorism itself should also be understood as an assault on basic rights. In all cases, the fight against terrorism must be respectful to human rights. Our Constitution laid down clear limitations on state actions within the context of the fight against terrorism. To maintain this delicate balance by protecting 'core' human rights is the responsibility of courts in a matter like this."

Laws to counter terrorism should not violate basic human rights, but should safeguard human rights, strengthen democracy and uphold the rule of law. In the case of D.K. Basu *v* State of West Bengal,[42] the Supreme Court held that: "State terrorism is no answer to combat terrorism. State terrorism would only provide legitimacy to terrorism that would be bad for the state, the community and above all for the rule of law. The state must, therefore, ensure that the various agencies deployed by it for combating terrorism act within the bounds of law and not become law unto themselves."

Conclusion

To fight the menace of terrorism in the true sense, the focus should not only to punish terrorists but efforts must also be made to ascertain the factors responsible for such acts. The government must pay attention to determine the causes which give rise to terrorism and try to eliminate those causes. Unfortunately despite the fact that the India is facing the problem of terrorism almost since independence, it has failed to systematise its approach to tackle the problem, over the past decades, terrorism activities have spread throughout the Indian territory, and our responses to the menace of terrorism are trapped in the same senseless cycle of enacting draconian laws. The Indian institutional structure of governance are repeating the pre-independence attitude to crush everything through harsh laws. Anti-terror legislations in independent India are completely out of sense with changing demand and force structure, and the laws are similar to British rule mandates. Such a strict and narrow approach may help to eliminate affect of terrorism but will not eradicate the causes of terrorism. Thus, such activities may again surface with more determination. Therefore, a proper balance between the law and the interest of the society is needed to attain the required result, otherwise 'War Against Terrorism' will ever never be won.

Terrorism has imposed new structural challenges on law enforcement agencies which is to accommodate even at a conceptual level. India has to restrain from following the British legacy. Series of bomb blasts by the terrorists on the territory of India[43] once again made the Government to take a hasty decision in enacting the Indian Investigating Agency Act 2008 and Amendments in Unlawful Activities (Prevention) Act of 1967. The enactment of NIA Act 2008 and Amendments in Unlawful Activities (Prevention) Act of 1967 may be a welcome step, but a strict – anti-terrorism law is no answer to the problem of terrorism. The persistent enforcement of anti-terror laws and similar other laws over the last several decades has slowly and silently crumbled legal system and damaged democratic principles. Laws on their own will not prevent terrorist attacks. Legislations need to be supplemented by increased resources, better training and coordination between security agencies, and social inclusion so that the vulnerable section of the Indian society are dissuaded from retaliating against the majority.

Notes

1. See Ahmad Lufti, Blowback, China and the Afghan Arabs, *Issues And Studies*, vol. 37, no.1, 160-214 (2001); K.P.S. Gill & Ajai Sahini, *The Global Threat Of Terror: Ideological, Material and Political Linkages* (1st ed. 2002).
2. See, Kanti P. Bajpai, *Roots of Terrorism* 4 (1st ed. 2002) at 4.
3. See, Rajiv A. Kapur, *Sikh Separatism: The Politics of Faith* (1st ed. 1986); Kuldip Nayar, Khushwant Singh, *Tragedy of Punjab: Operation Blue Star and After* (1st ed. 1984); Sarab Jit Singh, *Operation Black Thunder: An Eyewitness Account of Terrorism in Punjab*, (2002).
4. See, Balraj Puri, *Kashmir Towards Insurgency* (1st ed. 1995); Sumantara Bose, *The Challenge in Kashmir,* (1st ed. 1997); Sisir Gupta, *Kashmir Dispute: A Study in Indo-Pak Relations*, (1st ed. 1996); K.M. Mathur, *Challenges to Police Human Rights and National Security*, (1st ed. 2003); Riyaz Punjabi, Kashmiri: The Bruised Identity, in *Perspectives on Kashmir: The Roots of Conflicts in South Asia,* 139 (Raju G.C. Thomas ed., Colorado, 1992).
5. See, Prakash Singh, *Kohima to Kashmir: On The Terrorist Trail*, (1st ed. 2001); Ajay K. Mehra, India's Naxal Puzzle, *Mainstream*, Vol. No. XLI, 7, (2003).
6. See, Udayon Mishra, *The Periphery Strikes Back: Challenges to the Nation-State in Assam and Nagaland*, (1st ed. 2000); B.G. Verghese, *India's Northeast Resurgent: Ethnicity, Insurgency, Governence, Development* (1st ed. 1996)
7. *Id,* See, Phanjoubam Tarapot, *Insurgency Movement in Northeastern India*, (1st ed. 1996); R. Vashum, *Indo-Naga Conflict: Problem And Resolution*, (1st ed. 2001).
8. See, N.C. Asthana AND Anjali Nirmal, *Terrorism, Insurgencies and Counterinsurgency Operations*, (1st ed. 2001).

9. Ninan Koshy, *The War on Terror: Reordering the World*, 36 (1st ed. 2002).
10. G.B. Reddy, Indian Legal Regime Relating to Prevention of Terrorism: *An Analysis,In Terrorism in South Asia*, 246 (A.S. Raju ed., 2004).
11. See, Anti Terrorism and Security Laws in India: A Report to the Association of the Bar of the City of New York on a research Project for the Committee on International Human Rights, (Jan. 5, 2007), www.nycbar.org/pdf/ABCNY_India_Report.pdf.
12. *Id.*
13. Kulwant Singh, Efficacy of the Terrorist and Disruptive Activities (Preventive), Act, 1987 – An Appraisal, in, *Global Terrorism: Socio-Politico and Legal Dimensions*, 311 (B.P. Singh Sehgal ed., 2000); Arnab Gosswami, *Combating Terrorism: The Legal Challenge*, 17 (1st ed. 2002).
14. Gopal Bhargava, *Human Rights: Concern of the Future*, 315 (1st ed. 2001).
15. See, NHRC *Annual Report* 54 (1994-95); R. Swaroop, *Cases and Material on TADA*, (1st ed. 1993)
16. See, Chintan Chandrachud, *The cases that India Forgot*, (2019)
17. Law Commission in its 173rd report brought the Prevention of Terrorism Bill, 2000.
18. Law Commission of India, *Working paper on Legislation to Combat Terrorism*, (2000).
19. *Id.*
20. *Id.*
21. *Id.*
22. Gosswami, *Supra* note 19, at 17.
23. J S Verma, *The New Universe of Human Rights*, (2004), p. 110.
24. J S Verma, *The New Universe of Human Rights*, (2004), p. 110.
25. See Rajeev Dhavan, POTO: An Assault on Democracy, *The Hindu*, November 16, 2001, at 12; See Gautam Navlakha, POTO: Taking the Lawless Road, *Economic and Political Weekly*, vol. 36, no. 49, 4522 (2001).
26. Preeti Verma, *The Terror of Pota and Other Security Legislations: A Report on the People's Tribunal on The Prevention of Terrorism Act and other Security Legislations*, 437-438 (1st ed. 2004).
27. See Justice V.R. Krishna Iyer, *Legally Speaking* (1st ed. 2002).
28. See, Commonwealth Human Rights Initiative, Submision to the Review Committee of POTA, (Sept. 23, 2004), www.Humanrightsinitiative.Org/Artres/Pota_Submission.Pdf); Supra note 17; Asia Pacific Human Rights Network, Prevention of Terrorism Act, 2002, Submission to Advisory Council of Jurists of Asia Pacific Forum (2004), http://www.asiapacificforum.net/jurists/references/terrorism/aphrn_india.pdf.
29. Koshy, *Supra* note 15, at 93.
30. (1994) 3 SCC 770.
31. *Ibid* 710.
32. 2002, Cr. LJ 3368 at PP 3375-76.

33. 2003 (10) SCALE 967.
34. 2014 (1) Bom CR (Cri) 135.
35. https://www.thehindu.com/news/national/other-states/nia-told-me-to-go-soft-in-malegaon-2008-blast-case-says-special-public-prosecutor-rohini-salian/article7354066.ece accessed on 10/10/2019.
36. Abdul Khader Kunju S, UAPA Cases - Does The NIA Act Affect The Federal System? Available at, https://www.livelaw.in/columns/uapa-cases—does-the-nia-act-affect-the-federal-system-151825
37. K.G. Kannabiran, The State as a Terrorist, *Express Magazine*, June 23, 1985.
38. NATIONAL HUMAN RIGHTS COMMISSION, *Annual Report 2000-20001,* p. 12.
39. AIR 1990 SC 1962.
40. Maj. Gen. R S Mehta ed., *International Encyclopaedia of Terrorism Laws* 866 (1st ed. 2007).
41. (2004) 9 SCC 580 at page 596.
42. JT 1997 (1) SC 1.
43. The attack on Indian Parliament and the Mumbai attack on 26-11-2008.

Chapter - 3

Cyber Terrorism in India and Legal Regime

Introduction

The brutal killings and the terror perpetrated by terrorists is a sad reality faced by a modern world, including India. The terrorist attacks occurring at an alarming rate is severely jeopardising the fundamental structures of a democratic state. Moreover, with the development of Information Communication Technology (ICT), a new form of terrorism that is cyber terrorism emerged and is more sophisticated than compared to the traditional one. Further, combating against the blatant and hidden acts of cyber terrorism is not a regular criminal justice-endeavour instead, it is a challenge to the state machinery. Many countries to combat the menace of cyber terrorism unlocked new gates to curtail the freedom of speech and expression, liberty, privacy and other fundamental rights. India, one of the world's largest democracies, enacted specific anti-terrorism laws to tackle the menace of terrorism and included a provision concerning cyber terrorism in the Information Technology Act. Thus, the aim of this chapter is to make an inquiry into the conceptual framework of cyber terrorism and highlights the Indian legal regime in response to the menace of cyber terrorism. The chapter further critically examines section 66F of the Information Technology Act to illustrate that section 66F is a severe provision, and is against the very structure of democracy and the rule of law.

With the growth and progress in the field of Information Communication Technology (ICT), the evil of terrorism also attained immense strength to perpetuate destructive activities.[1] The attack of September 11, on the United States America exhibited that terrorist organisations are operating with increasing complexity, audacity and lethality and has attained a new outlook.[2] Now territorial boundaries are not obstacles in perpetuating the terrorist activities.[3] The world is bleeding due to the ruthless temper of terrorism.[4] The inhumane terrorist activities are responsible for the massacre of the number of innocent people. The world has witnessed many terrorist attacks, such as an attack of the World Trade Centre, Mumbai bomb explosion to Boston Marathon Bomb Blast in the year 2013 and the Paris attack on 13th November 2015. Recently the terrorist attack on Sri Lanka in April 2019 has revealed that terrorists are against humanity and are inhumane. This menace is an assault on democratic society which is getting more dreadful with the advancement of science and technology.

The technologies had not only enabled our life more comfortable but also empowered terrorist groups to undermine security and inflict harm. For example, modern communication technologies from satellite phones to the internet has aided a decentralised structure of terrorist groups in marshalling their resources to increase terrorist activities throughout the world.[5] Such technologies facilitate the encryption of messages, provides critical access information, and scores of sites provide information concerning the creation of explosives and other destructible materials.[6] Thus, by exploiting the ability of the internet, the terrorists have magnified their disruptive power. From example, a unique feature of Osama bin Laden's Arab Afghan crusade was its capability to rearrange the operations rapidly from one place to another as the situation demanded.[7]

Reports in the year 1997 revealed that Arab Afghan not only played an active role in activities carried out by Algeria's GIA and Egypt's IG but also aided the Islamic Liberation Party (ILP) while conducting operations in Somalia. They relocated crusaders to Xinxiang Uighur Province in the Western part of China, to crusade a religious war against the Chinese regime. The attack on US embassies in Kenya and Tanzania by Al Qaeda demonstrated that the smooth and swift mobility of members of Al Qaeda from one place to another, and it becomes possible because of adaption and use of information technology by the new generation of terrorist organisations.[8]

The terrorists are exploiting the internet technology very efficiently in their favour, and many contemporary terrorist leaders are willing to adopt the latest technology not merely to inspire and motivate the young people to join the organisation but also to spread disruptive activities across the world. Such technological innovations have given extremists a great conduit to disseminate their rhetoric and strategies to a large extent of the population.[9] The traditional types of ethnic/nationalist and separatist as well as ideological group have not only joined various other organisations with less comprehensible nationalist or ideological motivations but also transformed their modus operandi by using new technologies and lethality in recent years. For such distinctive networking of different terrorist organisations and change in the modus operandi, the diffusion of information technology across the world, as well as increased and free movement across the international boundaries, are the two most significant factors.[10]

India has been the prime target of militancy and terrorist group. These terrorist groups apply new technologies to champion their cause in India. Moreover, these terrorist groups have acquired a considerable amount of weapons and established their relations with the terrorist groups based outside India. At present perhaps all the terrorist groups based in India have some links and allocate resources with international terrorist networks such as Al Qaeda[11]and their association with ISIS cannot be ruled out considering the global outreach of ISIS. Such a development raises pressing concerns for India.

Determined to combat terrorism, the Indian government enacted anti-terrorism laws from time to time. In the year 1985, the government passed the Terrorists and Disruptive Activities (Prevention) Act 1985 (TADA), which was followed by the Prevention of Terrorism Act, 2002, the Unlawful Activities Prevention Act, 1967 (UAPA) amended latest in 2019 and et al. With the emergence of cyber terrorism, the Indian government included few provisions in the Information Technology Act to combat the threat of cyber terrorism.

Concept of Cyber Terrorism

Like terrorism, there prevails no single comprehensive acceptable definition of the term cyber terrorism.[12] The reasons behind the lack of a universally recognised interpretation of cyber terrorism is the existence of view that cyber terrorism is nothing but cyber offence. The other viewpoint is cyber terrorism can be defined as destructive or disruptive activities by use of internet and computer to generate fear potentially comparable to that from a physical act of terrorism, and there is no difference between the cyber terrorism and terrorism.[13]

As per Collin, "Cyber Terrorism" is a combination of two elements: cyberspace and terrorism. And as cyber terrorism is a fusion of cybernetics and terror, it can be held that cyber terrorism is prearranged, politically abetted and manipulated attack against computer, computer systems, computer programs and data to create lawless, chaotic order in society by indiscernible and imperceptible malevolence group.[14] There are numerous definitions of cyber terrorism given by various scholars, but few definitions are discussed below for the understanding of the concept of cyber terrorism.

A CRS Report 2005 characterises the term cyber terrorism in a broader way and classifies it in two groups, one Effect based and second Intent-based. When consequence of computer attacks is so disruptive that it creates fear in the mind of people similar to those generated by traditional terrorist activity such a situation is called as Effect based cyber terrorism, and when unlawful or politically abetted computer attacks are targeted to threaten or coerce a government or people to endorse or favour a political ideology, or to cause socioeconomic loss it is known as Intent-based cyber terrorism.[15] In other words, cyber terrorism can be termed as an act of threatening the unity, sovereignty and security of the state and creating fear in the mind of people by the use of computers and the internet.

A broader and inclusive definition of "cyber terrorism" is given by Kevin G. Coleman of the Technolytics Institute. According to him, cyber terrorism is the deliberate use of disrupting activities, or the threat thereof, against computers and networks, intending to cause injury, to spread social, ideological, religious, political or similar subjects, or to threaten any person in prolongation of such objectives. Mark Pollitt defined cyber terrorism as which tends to associate the word with a deliberate attack with political purposes, directed against information systems management that can determine serious consequences against targets that are not in a state of war.

Thus, from the definition mentioned above, it can be concluded that cyber terrorism is the politically motivated use of information technology by subnational groups to threaten or cause violence to intimidate a wider audience and to gain an advantage in a terrorist action or strategy.

Advantages of Cyberterrorism

Internet became popular among terrorists because of various reasons. The first reason is its ability to amend messages as per the audiences[16]; secondly, the inexpensive and potentially high-quality presentation and dissemination of information across the world because all that is required is a personal computer with an internet connection, it reduces the economic burden as they need not buy weapons, like guns or explosives, or acquire transportation; and lastly, the ability to create an persuading image of ideological group.[17] The secretive nature of the terrorist activities is the toughest test for the state machinery and ultimate gain to the new generation terrorist. They are executing distributed, astute network arrangements and managing the operations of members spread all over the world. Not only they are broadcasting information, but also associating organisations and supporting their activities.[18]

Apart from these main reasons, the other reasons which make internet popular among the terrorists, for example, in many terrorist attacks through the internet, there may not be a cautioning indication, as one may not even be apprehended that such activity has occurred. Outbreaks on computer systems can go undetected even after accomplishment. A cyber-terrorist may have infiltrated the system countless times before the actual cataclysm takes place.[19]

Moreover, such an act may be time-bound analogous to a bomb timer, intended to accomplish the aim at a particular specified time.[20] Intelligence gathering of cyber terrorism is challenging and herculean task for the state machinery.[21] The luxury with which the terrorist attack is executed without any retaliation is one of the advantageous attributes of cyber technology appreciated by terrorist organisations. Indeed, every active terrorist organisation in the present era demonstrate their ability to exploit cyber technology either by propagating their ideologies on websites owned by them or by using or misusing cyber technologies to aid terrorist attack.[22]

Thus, it is quite challenging to reckon the ease and speed of terrorist groups to adopt and execute destructive cyber-attacks in the coming future. Therefore, a suitable inference can be drawn that ever-growing digital world, cyber technology and strength of the terrorist groups entails a constant review of cyber-attack assiduously and needs appropriate legal mechanism to combat this menace.

The competencies and preferred strategies of terrorist groups developed over time. The terrorist activities in the present-day are moulded by progress and development in the field of Information Communication Technology (ICT), which facilitates trans-national connectivity which gives rise to new eccentric options in terrorist approaches. Because of multidimensional transformation in communication and computer technologies, indeed, it can be determined that terrorists and their cohorts will use instead say misuse them comprehensively.[23] Contemporary eventualities have proven that the threat of cyber terrorism is not imaginary. The sectors of national importance such as aviation, healthcare and others are vulnerable to cyber-terror attack.

ICT helped terrorists in exercising a skill of shifting extreme plans. Even a terrorist organisation having moderate resources can exploit the defective security mechanism of the State by using expertise in computer science and allied subjects.[24] With the development of ICT terrorist organisation now transform their strategies with ease to achieve effective results.[25] They are always targeting soft and vulnerable targets by applying innovative tactics. The unpredictable terrorist approach over the last fifty years substantiates this fact. For example, starting with political killing in the early twentieth century, hijacking of planes by terrorist organisations in the decade of 1970s, executing attacks by car bombs in the era of 90s and amplifying mass killing of civilians by human bombs in last twenty years. Indeed, the most effective plan in the execution of the terrorist act was the transformation of passenger aeroplane as a lethal weapon by Al-Qaida in the year 2001.[26] With this history of evolving strategic techniques, analysts have guesstimated on myriad future of terrorist activities around the world. They also believe that terrorist in coming future not only procure but will not hesitate in using the weapon of mass destruction to destabilise the political order.

Cyber Terrorism: An Emergent Threat

Indeed, practices and predictions of terrorists acquiring destructive cyber capabilities date back many years. In the year 1990, the National Academy of Sciences alerted the first cyber-attack that is termed as 'Digital Pearl Harbour.'[27] A decade earlier cyber terrorism was very much in its infancy, but now this new mode of terrorism is emerged as a deadly threat leaving the world totally off guard; the approaches are fundamental and naive but worthwhile, patron-less destruction can be advanced with a much higher degree of efficiency through the internet technology.[28] Mark Potok, a Southern Poverty Law Centre analyst, viewed: "The internet is an important piece of the leaderless struggle approach. It permits lone wolves to keep well-informed of actions, alterations in ideology and discussions of tactics – all of which may impact his-own choice of target. Far more than hard copy publications the internet allow the lone-wolf to remain a part of a longer movement even though he attends no meetings, put his name on no lists, and generally try to remain invisible. A good example of this is Mathew Williams, the confessed murder of a gay couple in California, who used the internet to privately explore a variety of extremist ideologies before picking up the gun."[29]

A good number of terrorist groups listed by the US State department's list labelled maintain websites on the internet. While US official believes that some terrorists used encrypted e-mail to plan acts of terrorism, most of the group appear to use the internet to spread their propaganda.[30] In the year 1996, a US-based Internet Service Provider (ISP) was disabled by a computer hacker damaging part of its record-keeping system and signed off with the threat, "you have yet to see true electronic terrorism. This is a promise." The Spanish protestors in the year 1998, bombarded the Institute for Global Communication (IGC) by thousands of bogus email because they demanded the IGC should stop hosting a website for the Euskal Herria Journal, a New York-based publication supporting Basque in independence (Mali, 2012).[31] The ethnic guerrillas swamped Sri Lankan embassies with hundreds of e-mails per day and the message read "We are the internet black Tigers and are going to disrupt communication." It is said to be the first known attack by terrorists against a country's computer system. NATO computers were blasted with e-mails and hit by denial of service attacks during the Kosovo conflict in 1999.[32]

Some militant organisations also use the internet to propagate anti-western, anti-Israel objectives. Hezbollah manages at least three websites. One for the central press office at www.hizbollah.org, the organisation, sells books and publications with the help of these websites. Other sites, www.moqawama.org and www.almanar.co.ib, were used to describe its attacks on Israeli targets, to broadcast the news and information and to make available information on how to make bombs as well as for instructions for making hazardous chemical and explosives weapons. There were also websites devoted to bin Laden and jihadists sites, such as London based azzam.com, which deliver a wide range of products and services.[33] A degree of the site's global reach can be comprehended in response to the death of a Saudi named Khallal al-Madani, who was killed in Chechnya in February 2000 while fighting under the command of bin Laden. Within a day, messages for sustenance for al-Madani's family was received from several parts of the world.[34] Chechen groups also maintained websites in more than twelve languages, from Albanian to Swedish.[35]

Terrorist groups are harnessing the technology to meet their end. They are using internet technology to design plans, to raise funds, to propagate their ideologies and persuade the younger generation to join the camp.[36] Indeed, such menace will rise in coming time as the leadership positions in terrorist organisations are increasingly filled with internet-savvy people."[37] In the year 2017, ISIS put out a call to their recruits focussed on civilians in Europe, the US, Australia and even in India. This call was fulfilled with attacks in Manchester, London, France, and a bomb attempt in Brussels during the summer of 2017.[38]

Moreover, the terrorist groups are trying to increase the use of cryptocurrency to dodge traditional black market terror financing operations, as crypto-funding of terror activities advances added peril.[39] The fact that ISIS has four online media publications apart from sophisticated online posts, video, tweets and retweets raise the apprehension for the world to focus on cyber technology to control their impact on the population.[40]

Cyber Terrorism in India

Cyber terrorism in India is no longer an illusion.[41] On 2nd April 2002, the Anti India Crew (A.I.C) of Pakistan had infected the websites of India and tried to destroy and delete the entire information stored in the computer, computer system or computer network of eighty-eight websites including the websites of Indian government.[42] The horrific 26/11 Mumbai attack is a glaring example wherein the use of ICT by terrorist made it quite difficult for Indian security forces to differentiate and capture these perpetrators.[43] On 13th July 2010, the ICT was exploited in Zaveri bomb blast. In 2010 Varanasi bomb blast ICT was utilised for communication, Indian Mujahidin took the responsibility of the explosion through email, which was traced to WiFi connection in the Vashi, Navi Mumbai.[44] Virtual SIMs were used by Jaish Mohammad suicide bomber in the Pulwama attack in Jammu and Kashmir on 14th February 2019.[45] The cyberspace has eventually become the platform for cyberwar and terrorist activity. The terrorist organisation appreciates cyber-attacks an effective mechanism of jihad in executing crusade against their enemies. Terrorist groups have developed their abilities to abuse the virtual world.

Cybersecurity and war experts Singer and Friedman assert that even though there is a massive number of research articles discussing the phenomenon of cyber terrorism but the world has not seen any physical injury or killing by cyber terrorism.[46] India also has yet not experienced any occurrence of substantial cyber-attack which can be designated as terrorism. However, this does not mean that the terrorist groups will not abuse cyberspace to inflict death and destruction, as there is a considerable increase in the number of talented and ambitious terrorist groups capable of severely causing cyber-attacks in any part of the world.[47]

The terrorist organisations by decentralised network arrangements are managing the activities of members spread all over the world. Not only they are broadcasting information, but also associating organisation and supporting their businesses.[48] Indeed, every active terrorist organisation in the present era demonstrate their ability to exploit cyber technology either by propagating their ideologies on websites owned by them or by using or misusing cyber technologies to aid terrorist attack,[49] and it is quite challenging to reckon the ease and speed of terrorist groups to adopt and execute destructive cyber-attacks in coming future. Therefore, a suitable inference can be drawn that in an ever-growing digital world, cyber technology and strength of the terrorist groups entails a constant review of cyber-attack assiduously and needs appropriate legal mechanism to combat this menace in India.

Legal Regime to Combat Cyber Terrorism in India

The problem of terrorism in India is not new, but after independence from British rule and more specifically during the decade of the 1980s, the situation became worst. The Indian Government to combat terrorism enacted its first anti-terrorism law Terrorist, and Disruptive Activities (Preventive) Act, 1985 (TADA), which was repealed in 1995. In the year 2002, the second anti-terrorism law Prevention of Terrorism Act (POTA) was enacted. The life of POTA was short; it lasted nearly a year. Both these laws were against the basic principle of criminal justice and drastically failed to tackle the grave situation created by terror groups. After the repeal of POTA, provisions to curb the menace of terrorism was enshrined in Unlawful Activities and (Prevention) Act 1967 (UPAA) after necessary amendments, but no rules were included to tackle cyber terrorism.

Even though the threat of cyber-terrorist attacks is no more a myth, the Indian government has not enacted any specific cyber-terrorist legislation to combat this menace. In the year 2000, the Indian government legislated the Information Technology Act, 2000 (IT Act). Further, this enactment was legislated primarily to acknowledge e-commerce and to facilitate electronic filing of documents with the Government agencies. However, the Act (Chapter XI) lists few offences relating to the use and abuse of computer system which invites a penalty or imprisonment or both.[50]

The IT Act included the offences such as hacking, cyber obscenity, tampering with computer and data, misrepresentation before the Controller of Certifying Authorities or his assistants, breach of confidentiality and privacy, publication of false digital signature certificate. However, but cyber-offences such as cyber-stalking, cyber-theft and even cyber-defamation were not punished under this Act. Thus, the IT Act was an incomplete code dealing with few specific cyber-offence. The reason for excluding several cyber offences may be the perception that the provisions of Indian Penal Code 1862 and other penal statutes are sufficient enough to tackle cyber issues. However, time belied such impression and the fast growth rate of cybercrimes and especially cyber terrorism compelled the government to expand the spectrum of the IT Act 2000. While the government has embarked on a variety of legal initiatives to protect against the threat of terrorism, a growing number of issues related to cyber terrorism remain unanswered.

The size and nature of cybercrime and the menace of cyber terrorism in India compelled the Indian government to reformulate the Information Technology Act 2000. Thus, in December 2008 as a spontaneous reaction against the Mumbai terror attack, the Information Technology (Amendments) Act, 2008 was hastily presented before the Parliament and was passed in one go without any debate whatsoever. The vital concern of the new Information Technology Act, 2008 was on cybercrime and to a substantial degree on cyber Terrorism.

Section 66F firmly dealt with the issue of cyber terrorism by defining and severely punishing such an offence. Several other provisions were introduced by the Amendment Act 2008, which may be related to cyber terrorism appeared to be a good and welcome step by the Government to fight against dreadful evil. Section 70 A and Section 70 B of the Act aims to protect the critical infrastructure of the country and essential defence and scientific installations, these two sections cover the investigatory process and at times can be used as a preventive measure too. It is a well-accepted fact that terrorists are now using cloaking devices provided by encryption companies to keep security agencies from reading their communication.[51]

Consequently, the Indian government under section 69 of the IT Act can authorise any government authority to intercept, monitor or decrypt any information generated, transmitted or stored in any computer resource. The state security is endangered not only by terrorists but by the surveillance by the States or entities who supported such evil activities. Thus, the Government is empowered under section

69-A to block access of any information from the public if there lies any reasonable apprehension to breach of security.

Further, the new eventualities of cybersecurity alarm like wiki leaks etc. perhaps stimulated India to implement the National Cyber Security Policy, 2013. This policy aims to protect the cybersecurity of the state, although it is not a statute but a welcome step to deal with the issues related to cybersecurity and cyber-terrorism.[52]

No doubt, (cyber) terrorism is the real threat to the present society, and it is the principal obligation of the government in a democratic rule to afford protection and security to the people of the nation and in achieving such objective the governments are free to take all such essential and necessary actions they think appropriate.[53] But in doing so the state has to be very careful, care must be taken so that innocent people are not harassed, and their fundamental rights are not violated as all laws derive strength not only from the authority of the State but also from the support of the people. As the physical correction is not merely in-laws; it is much more in the vibrant functioning of the administrative and political institutions.[54]

Inequality before the law or economic, social-political, cultural factors and even uneven application of the law must come to an end as these factors fuel the terrorism.[55] An analysis of section 66F illustrates that the provision under section 66F is against the democratic rule and can be misused by state machinery as was in the case of section 66-A of the IT Act. The Supreme Court in case of Shreya Singhal *v* Union of India[56]while declaring section 66-A unconstitutional observed that like section 66-A, section 66F is another narrowly drawn section, but unfortunately the Supreme Court has not dealt with the issue relating to section 66F as it was not raised before the Court by the petitioner.

Critical Analysis of Section 66F

An analysis of the definition of cyber terrorism as defined under section 66F reveals that the impugned definition is ambiguous, unreasonable and broad enough to cover any act concerning to internet within the ambit of Cyber Terrorism. Such a loose definition opens the floodgate for arbitrary and selective application by the state machinery.[57] It provides state agencies with ample opportunity to harass and exploit any person. Section 66 F embodies the principle expressed in the rule of '*actus reus not facit nisi mens sit rea*', that is, both guilty intention and criminal act are necessary to constitute the offence of cyber terrorism.

However, as the crime or prosecution is based on the interpretation of the law enforcer's intent behind that action when the police suspect a person of having a particular intention, this section can be invoked, and the person has to spend years in jail before the judiciary decides whether he is guilty of having that intention or not.[58] For example, in case of Niranjan Singh Karan Singh *v* Jitendra Bhimraj Bijjaya[59] the accused was charged under section 3 of TADA on the fact that they killed their opponents with intent to strike terror in the people or segment of people (residents of the locality) with the use of weapons such as knives and iron rods. The Apex Court held that though the result of such acts is bound to create panic and fear, but the intention of committing the offence cannot be said to strike terror in the people or any section of society as defined under section 3 of TADA. A mere statement to the effect that shows of such violence would create violence in terror or fear in the minds of people and as a consequence of which none would dare to oppose them, is not sufficient to constitute an offence under section 3(1) of the Act.

Though the accused got the relief from the Supreme Court, it shows how state agencies were empowered with arbitrary power to charge any person under TADA who had committed the offence under another penal statute. This conclusion is further substantiated by numerous other cases that have occurred during the draconian regime of POTA.[60] The experience creates apprehension that section 66F can be misused by state machinery in the like manner. Moreover, the application of section 66FA in a matrimonial case is a glaring example of how an ordinary member of the society can misuse it. However, the trial proceedings for offences under section 498A, 506, 384, 120B of Indian Penal Code and section 3 and 4 of Dowry Prohibition Act and sections 66A, 66F of the IT Act was quashed by the Karnataka High Court.[61]

Another eye-catching fact in this definition is its resemblance with clause (2) of Article 19 of the Indian Constitution.[62] Article 19 (2) of the Constitution stipulates the parameters up to which the freedom of speech and expression can be legally restrained. Article 19 (2) of the

Constitution authorises the legislature to impose reasonable restraint on the right to freedom of speech and expression enshrined under Article 19 (1)(a) of the Constitution of India. The reasonable constraint can be enforced on the grounds mentioned under Article 19 (2) such as security of the state, friendly relations with foreign countries, public order, decency and morality, contempt of court, defamation, incitement of offence and sovereignty and integrity of India. These reasonable restrictions can only be imposed through enacted legislation and by executive order.[63]

Further section 66F states that any person knowingly or intentionally penetrates or accesses a computer resource without authorization or exceeding authorized access, and by means of such conduct obtains access to such information, data or computer database that is restricted for reasons for the security of the State or foreign relations, or any restricted information, data or computer database, with reason to believe that such information, data or computer database so obtained may be used to cause or likely to cause injury to the interest of the sovereignty and integrity of India, the security of the State, friendly relations with foreign States, public order, decency or morality, or in relation to contempt of court, defamation or incitement to an offence, or to the advantage of any foreign nation, group of individuals or otherwise, commits the crime of cyber terrorism. In other words, grounds mentioned under Article 19(2) restricting the right freedom of speech and expression can be characterised as cyber terrorism if any person knowingly or intentionally does any act prohibited under section 66F of the IT Act.[64] In other words, Article 19(2) read with section 66 F of the IT Act is cyber terrorism.

The other objectionable term used in this section is defamation, contempt of court and decency or morality how these terms are related to cyber terrorism is not backed by any reasonable logic. Even, the offence of defamation and contempt of court were outside the spectrum of 'Terrorist Activities' under TADA and Prevention of Terrorism Act 2002. Furthermore, Unlawful Activities and (Prevention) Act 1967, which defines 'Terrorist Act' does not include defamation and contempt of court within the definition of terrorist activities.

According to section 2 of the Contempt of Courts Act, 1971, the term 'contempt of court' means civil or criminal contempt. For civil contempt, there should be willful disobedience to any judgment, decree, direction, order, writ or other processes of a court or deliberate breach of an undertaking given to the court. Further contempt of court will be a criminal contempt if the publication of any matter or any act scandalizes or tends to offend, or lowers or tend to reduce the authority or dignity of any court or prejudices, or interferes or tends to interfere with the due course of judicial proceeding or in any manner interferes or tends to interfere with or obstruct or tends to impede the administration of justice.[65] The Supreme Court and the High Court are authorised to punish people for contempt of court under Article 129 and 215 of the Constitution, respectively. Section 10 of the Contempt of Court Act 1971, empowers the High Court to punish any person for contempt of its subordinate courts.

The contempt of court is a concept having a legacy of Anglo-Saxon jurisprudence. The purpose behind the contempt of court is that the court should not become powerless in the face of disobedience of its order by the executive and with no other means of implementing its directive.[66] It is a mechanism which the people themselves have given the courts and which courts keep properly sheathed to be used rarely but only when the public demands it.

To ensure that the task of judiciary to maintain harmony and balance between the different parts of the government which is necessary for the growth and sustenance of democracy is not defeated Article 19(2) provides that right to speech and expression guaranteed under Article 19(1)(a) is subject to the state making any law in relation to any contempt of courts. However, an enactment about contempt which imposes an unreasonable restriction on the right of the citizens to freedom of speech and expression would be *pro tanto* ultra-vires.[67]

Moreover, it must be acknowledged that contempt is a matter between the court and the contemnor and state has no role to play in determining that a person has committed an act of contempt or not.[68] The earlier anti-terrorism law in India and even present anti-terrorism law (UPAA 1967) do not put contempt of court within the spectrum terrorism, but while defining cyber terrorism under section 66(F) contempt of court is well within the ambit of the terrorist act.

Reputation of a man is as valuable as physical safety, property and any valuable security. It is rightly said that if money is lost nothing is lost but if reputation is lost everything is lost. The defamation hurts a man's reputation.[69] Therefore, section 499 of the Indian Penal Code defines and punishes the act of defamation. Section 499 states that in order that an offence of defamation is committed there must be making or publication of any imputation concerning any person by words either spoken or intended to be read or by signs or by visible representation expecting to harm or knowing or having reason to believe that such imputation will harm the reputation of such person.[70] The essence of the offence of defamation is the publication of the imputation with the knowledge that it will harm the reputation of the person defamed.[71]

Every citizen in India has a right to criticise the corrupt government without fear of litigation, as Article 19(1) provides the freedom of speech and expression with reasonable restriction. In the case of City of Chicago *v* Tribune Co.[72] Thompson CJ of the Supreme Court of Illinois observed that: 'Every citizen has the right to criticise an inefficient or corrupt government without fear of civil or criminal prosecution. This absolute privilege is founded on the principle that it is advantageous for the public interest that the citizen should not be in any way fettered in his statement, and where the public service or due administration of justice is involved, he shall have the right to speak his mind freely, the government, local authority and other organs of State, exercising governmental powers cannot maintain a suit for damages for defaming them.'

An individual officeholder may, however, agitate, if defamed, individually, but 'state' as such cannot sue a citizen on its behalf. This rule was established in the United States[73] and in the United Kingdom this rule was created through Derbyshire County Council *v* Times Newspaper Ltd.[74]and accepted in India in case of Raj Gopal *v* State of Tamil Nadu.[75] However, in case of New York *v* Sullivan,[76] it was observed that a public official if he feels offended by defamatory article could sue and recover damages for defamatory, false statement concerning to his official conduct unless the speech was made with the knowledge that it was a fake and reckless disregard of whether it was true or false. Right to disapprove on matters of government and politics in Australia has been held to be an indispensable incident of the representative government under Constitution, which explicitly contains no fundamental rights. By putting the offence of defamation within the ambit of Cyber Terrorism means that writing anything which is not suitable to the government amounts to cyber terrorism, which otherwise is no offence and such a provision is subject to abuse.[77]

Decency or morality again has no nexus with cyber terrorism. Decency can be defined as a lack of obscenity. No person can be allowed to deteriorate and dilapidate the social structure and morality of the society, and for that reason, any obscenity should be suppressed and punished.[78] Further, the conception of morality differs from place to place and from time to time.[79] For example, birth control and contraceptives were once considered immoral and taboo, and indeed, there have been convictions for publishing literature dealing with contraception.[80] But, today, in the modern world, the outlook has transformed, and it is no more a taboo to discuss such matters. Instead, the State, by itself, encourages and promotes the use of contraceptives. Sometimes an act might be 'morally offensive' to one person need not be so to another person; the conduct is moral or immoral depends entirely on each person's culture and society he belongs.[81] This further buttresses the argument that the expression used in section 66(F) are vague and ambiguous.

Thus, the expression used in section 66F such as 'Contempt of Court', 'Defamation' 'Decency or Morality' and 'Public Order' are vague, elastic and general and in the absence of any precise definition, limitation or clarification as to extent and scope of each of the expressions, it is impossible for a reasonable man to ascertain whether his conduct is outside the scope of 66F or not.

Moreover, the legislature has not looked beyond section 43 and section 66 to address the offences like cyber terrorism.[82] The term "computer contaminant" used in section 66 F is to have the same connotation as given in section 43 of the Act, meaning thereby that any act which falls under section 43 is also covered under section 66F of the Act. Moreover, section 66 of the IT Act states that if any person, dishonestly or fraudulently does any act referred to in section 43, he shall be punishable. It means that section 43 and section 66, both sections are covered under section 66F with graver punishment.[83] Therefore, enactment of such a patently vague provision is wholly unjustified and having the horrific past of experience of TADA and

POTA has led to a situation where it is impossible to believe that having such an extensive provision cannot be misused by state machinery against any person.

Thus, section 66F suffers from the iniquity of elusiveness because the expression mentioned therein bear different consequences in a given situation and depends on the subjective opinion of the statutory authority without any objective standard or norm.[84] In the context of the internet, the enforcement of section 66F is a treacherous form of suppression which is not authorised by the Constitution of India. Defining the offence concerning the medium employed for communication leads to arbitrariness. For example, an identical interface in a physical form would not be subjected to penal action. However, the same interface over an electronic platform exposes the person to criminal liability. Hence, it widens the scope of misuse of power by the state administration. Such provisions merely weaken the faith of people in democratic system as such provision which was hastily designed to combat cyber terrorism might be easily hijacked to fundamental rights and freedoms by the state machinery thus, if any provision which derogates the fundamental rights of any person and is unreasonable and unfair such provision should be deleted from the statute book.

Conclusion

In brief, it may be concluded that cyber terrorism is undoubtedly being one of the gravest threat in the present era and as terrorists are going for more lethal weapons and that their outlook of killing one and frightening hundreds is now transformed with time. They are of the view that killing more and more will make them win in the directionless war. Their nature has now become more lethal, and with the technological advancement, in the society, they too are benefited and are exploiting the new technology to create chaos and fearful environment. In light of such a grave situation, it is the primary responsibility of the democratic state to provide protection and security to the people and consequently can enact a statute to curb down the menace of cyber terrorism. But in doing so the country has to be very cautious, care must be taken so that innocent people are not beleaguered and their fundamental rights are not dishonoured as all laws derive strength not only from the authority of the state but also from the support of the people.[85] There should be a balance between the security concern and human rights considerations. The regulatory and monitoring mechanisms, which help to deter, identify, and track terrorists have to be there, but these should not jeopardise the liberty and freedom of the citizens.[86]

The impossibility of trying to restraint terrorism while not jeopardizing human rights, to some extent cannot be denied; but, there is a note of caution; the higher the power, the more dangerous the abuse, abuse of laws cannot altogether be ruled out, but if the misuse happens on the larger scale, it could be onslaught on the democratic rule of law.[87] The Highest Court of India in case of Niranjan Singh Karan Singh Punjabi *v.* Jitendra Bhimraj[88]observed: "When a law visits a person with serious penal consequences extra care must be taken to ensure that those whom the legislature did not intend to be covered by the express language of the statute are not roped in by stretching the language of the law." Further, Burke had rightly expressed his just apprehension more than two and half centuries ago in his letter to Hon. C.J. Fox (8 Oct. 1777), "People crushed by law have no hopes but from power. If laws are their enemies, they will be enemies to laws; and those, who have much to hope and nothing to lose, will always be dangerous, more or less". It is a well-accepted fact that security of the society is undisputable the primary aim of a welfare state, but it is not the sole purpose, one of the most significant and foremost duties of the states is to protect the fundamental rights guaranteed in the Constitution. It would be ironic if, in the name of combating (cyber) terrorism, the rule of law is kept aside, and the state violates the rights of the citizens. Hence section 66F needs reconsideration as this section is a disproportionate and discriminatory reaction to the menace of cyber terrorism. It is excessive and unfair as section 66F covers such acts which have no cogent nexus with cyber terrorism.

Notes

1. Gilbert Ramsay, Conceptualising Online Terrorism, *Terrorism Research Initiative*, Vol. 2, No. 7. pp. 3-10.
2. Sanjay Gupta, The Changing Dimensions of International Terrorism and the Role of the United States: A Comprehensive and Multilateral Approach to Combat

Global Terrorism, *The Indian Journal of Political Science*, Vol. 65. No. 4 (2004), pp. 556-587.

3. *Ibid;* Mahapatra,&Tripathy. (Eds.). *Transnational Terrorism: Perspectives on Motives, Measures and Impacts* (2007)
4. Adrian Guelke, *The New Age of Terrorism and the International Political System* (2010).
5. Mates Michael. *Report: Technology and Terrorism. NATO Parliamentary Assembly, 2001*. Retrieved on 2019, December 19 fromhttp://www.naa.be/archivedpub/comrep/2001/au-221-e.asp; See also, Oh, O., Agrawal, M & Rao, H.R. (2011) Information control and terrorism: Tracking the Mumbai terrorist attack through twitter. *Information Systems Frontiers,* "Special Issue on Terrorism Informatics", *13*(1), 33-43.
6. Robertson E. Ann, *Terrorism and Global Security*, (2007).
7. Kaplan David. (2003, June 2). Playing Offense: The inside story of How US Terrorist Hunters are Going After Al-Qaeda.*US News and World Report.*
8. *Ibid.*; See also, Jerrold M. Post, Kevin G. Ruby & Eric D. Shaw, From Car Bombs to Logic Bombs: The Growing Threat From Information Terrorism, Vol 12(2) (Terrorism and Political Violence, Summer 2000)
9. Minei. Elizabeth. Matusitz Jonathan. (2012). Cyberspace as a New Arena for Terroristic Propaganda: An Updated Examination. *Poiesis Prax,* 9: 163-176.
10. Martin Gus. *Understanding terrorism: challenges Perspective and Issues*, (2006).
11. Kamath, P.M. (2001) Terrorism in India: Impact on National Security, *Strategic Analysis*, vol. 25, no. 9; Gunaratna, Rohan. (September 16, 2002) Next Stop for Al-Qaida, *The Times Of India.*
12. Sanjay Gupta, The Changing Dimensions of International Terrorism and the Role of the United States: A Comprehensive and Multilateral Approach to Combat Global Terrorism, *The Indian Journal of Political Science*, Vol. 65. No. 4 (2004), pp. 556-587;
13. Foggetti, Nadina. (2010). Cyber Terrorism and The Right to Privacy in the Third Pillar Perspective, *Masaryk University Journal of Law and Technology*, Vol. 3: 3.
14. Collin C. Barry. (1996).*The Future of Cyber Terrorism. Proceedings of the 11th Annual International Symposium on Criminal Justice Issues. The University of Illinois at Chicago*. Retrieved March 23, 2019, fromhttp://stinet.ditc.mil/cgibin/GetTRDoc?ADA439217&Location=U2&doc=GetTRDoc. Seel also, Addicot F.Jeffrey, *Terrorism Law: Materials, Cases, Comments*, (2011).
15. Addicot F.Jeffrey, *Terrorism Law: Materials, Cases, Comments*, (2011).
16. Michael Whine, "Islamist Organisations on the Internet", Draft circulated on the Internet, April 1998, at www.ict.org/il/articles; See also,
17. *Ibid.*
18. *Ibid.*
19. Stytz, Martin. Banks Sheila. (2014). Towards Attaining Cyber Dominance. *Strategic Studies Quarterly*. Vol. 8 No. 1. pp. 55-87.
20. Mahapatra,&Tripathy. (Eds.), *Transnational Terrorism: Perspectives on Motives, Measures and Impacts*, (2007).

21. Griset L. Pamala, & Mahan Sue. (Eds.), *Terrorism in Perspective*, (2003).
22. Hoffman Bruce, *Inside terrorism*, (2006); Seel also, Weimann Gabriel, *Terror on the Internet*, (2006).
23. Martin Gus, *Understanding terrorism: challenges Perspective and Issues*, (2006).
24. Stytz, Martin. Banks Sheila. (2014). Towards Attaining Cyber Dominance. *Strategic Studies Quarterly*. Vol. 8 No. 1. Pp. 55-87.
25. Sanjay Gupta, The Changing Dimensions of International Terrorism and the Role of the United States: A Comprehensive and Multilateral Approach to Combat Global Terrorism, *The Indian Journal of Political Science*, Vol. 65. No. 4 (2004), pp. 556-587.
26. Ramsay, Gilbert. (April 2008). Conceptualising Online Terrorism, *Terrorism Research Initiative*, Vol. 2, No. 7. pp. 3-10.
27. Weimann Gabriel. (2000). *Cyberterrorism: How Real is the Threat?* United States Institute of Peace Special report.
28. See, John K. Klein, Deterring and Dissuading Cyberterrorism, *Journal of Strategic Security*, Vol. 8. No. 4, pp. 23-38.
29. Griset L. Pamala, & Mahan Sue. (Eds.), *Terrorism in Perspective*,. (2003).
30. Ramsay, Gilbert. (April 2008). Conceptualising Online Terrorism, *Terrorism Research Initiative*, Vol. 2, No. 7. pp. 3-10.
31. Michael Whine, "Islamist Organisations on the Internet", Draft circulated on the Internet, April 1998, at www.ict.org/il/articles.
32. See, John K. Klein, Deterring and Dissuading Cyberterrorism, *Journal of Strategic Security*, Vol. 8. No. 4, pp. 23-38.
33. Ramsay, Gilbert. (April 2008). Conceptualising Online Terrorism, *Terrorism Research Initiative*, Vol. 2, No. 7. pp. 3-10.
34. Bergen L. Peter, *Holy War, Inc.: Inside the Secret World of Osama bin Laden*, (2001).
35. *Ibid*; See also, Addicot F. Jeffrey, *Terrorism Law: Materials, Cases, Comments*, (2011).
36. Ramsay, Gilbert. (April 2008). Conceptualising Online Terrorism, *Terrorism Research Initiative*, Vol.2, No. 7. pp. 3-10
37. Griset L. Pamala, & Mahan Sue. (Eds.), *Terrorism in Perspective*,. (2003).
38. Oz Sultan, Tackling Disinformation, Online Terrorism, and Cyber Risks into the 2020s. Available at https://cyberdefensereview.army.mil/Portals/6/5_SULTAN_CDR_V4N1.pdf?ver=2019-04-30-105203-250
39. *Ibid.*
40. *Ibid.*
41. Indian Risk Survey. (2018). Available at http://ficci.in/Sedocument/20450/India%20Risk%20Survey%20-%202018.pdf.
42. S.R. Bhansli, *Commentary on Information Technology Act,* (2012); See also, Saxena, A. (August 4, 2011) 117 Indian Government Websites Defaced Till July. MEDIANAMA. Available at, http://medianama.com/2011/08/223-indian-government-websites-hacked/, Accessed on 17th August 2019.

43. Oh, O., Agrawal, M & Rao, H.R. (2011) Information control and terrorism: Tracking the Mumbai terrorist attack through twitter. *Information Systems Frontiers,* "Special Issue on Terrorism Informatics", *13*(1), 33-43.
44. See, Mathiha & Aswathy, A critical Study on Cyber Terrorism with Reference with 26/11 Mumbai Attack, *IJPAM*, Vol. 119, No. 17. pp. 1617-1636.
45. See, The Hindu, 24th March 2019.
46. P.W. Singer and Allan Friedman, *Cybersecurity and Cyberwar: What Everyone Needs to Know*, (2014); See also, Ramsay, Gilbert. (April 2008). Conceptualising Online Terrorism, *Terrorism Research Initiative*, Vol.2, No. 7. pp. 3-10.
47. Oz Sultan, Tackling Disinformation, Online Terrorism, and Cyber Risks into the 2020s. Available at https://cyberdefensereview.army.mil/Portals/6/5_SULTAN_CDR_V4N1.pdf?ver=2019-04-30-105203-250.
48. Michael Whine, "Islamist Organisations on the Internet", Draft circulated on the Internet, April 1998, at www.ict.org/il/articles.
49. Hoffman Bruce, *Inside terrorism*, (2006); Weimann Gabriel, *Terror on the Internet*, (2006).
50. See, Mathiha & Aswathy, A critical Study on Cyber Terrorism with Reference with 26/11 Mumbai Attack, *IJPAM*, Vol. 119, No. 17. pp. 1617-1636.
51. Stytz, Martin. Banks Sheila. (2014). Towards Attaining Cyber Dominance. *Strategic Studies Quarterly*. Vol.8 No. 1. Pp. 55-87.
52. Desai. Dhaval, Bhatt. Parjanya. (2019). 'Securing India's Cities: Remembering 26/11, Learning its Lesson'. *ORF Special Report*. No. 92. July 2019.
53. Debarati Halder, Information Technology Act and Cyber Terrorism: A Critical Review, P. Madhava Soma Sundaram (Ed.), *Cyber Crime and Digital Disorder*, (2011).
54. See, NHRC Report 2000-2001.
55. Foggetti, Nadina. (2010). Cyber Terrorism and The Right to Privacy in the Third Pillar Perspective, *Masaryk University Journal of Law and Technology*, Vol. 3: 3.
56. (2015) 5 SCC.
57. Mohanty Amlan. (2011). New Crimes Under the Information Technology (Amendment Act, *The Indian Journal of Law and Technology*, vol. 7. pp. 103-120.
58. See, Arun Shourie, *Courts and their Judgments*, (2018).
59. (1990) 4 SCC 76.
60. Singh Prakash, Terrorism and the Rule of Law. In N.R. Madhava Menon (Ed.), *Rule of Law in a Free Society*, (2008).
61. See, Pavan M. *v* State, CRIMINAL PETITION NO.1247/2013.
62. Nappinai. NS., *Technology Decoded*, (2017).
63. Express Newspaper (P) Ltd. *v* Union of India (1986) 1 133; Bijoe Emmanuel *v* State of Kerala (1986) 3 SCC 615.
64. Nappinai. NS., *Technology Decoded*, (2017).
65. Venugopal. K.K, Subramanium, Gopal, *Restatement of Indian Law of Contempt of Court*, (2011).

66. Reddy, O. Chinnapa, *The Court and the Constitution of India*, (2010).
67. See, E.M.S. Namoodaripad *v* T. Nayayanan Nambiar, (1970) 2 SCC 325.
68. Venugopal. K.K, Subramanium, Gopal, *Restatement of Indian Law of Contempt of Court*, (2011).
69. See, M.C. Verghese *v* T.J. Punnam, 1970 CriLJ 1651: AIR 1970 SC 1876.
70. *Ibid.*
71. See, Wahid Ullah *v* Emperor, AIR 1935 All 743.
72. (1923) 307 ILL 595, p 607.
73. See, New York *v* Sullivan (1964) 376 US 254.
74. (1993) 1All ER 1011 (HL).
75. AIR 1995 SC 264, p. 277.
76. (1964) 376 US 254
77. Nappinai. NS., *Technology Decoded*, (2017).
78. Rajak. Brajesh, *Pornography Law*, (2011).
79. *Ibid.*
80. See, R *v* Bradlaugh, 3 QBD 607.
81. Rajak. Brajesh, *Pornography Law*, (2011).
82. Mohanty Amlan. (2011). New Crimes Under the Information Technology (Amendment Act, *The Indian Journal of Law and Technology*, vol. 7. pp. 103-120.
83. Debarati Halder, Information Technology Act and Cyber Terrorism: A Critical Review, P. Madhava Soma Sundaram (Ed.), *Cyber Crime and Digital Disorder*, (2011).
84. Mohanty Amlan. (2011). New Crimes Under the Information Technology (Amendment Act, *The Indian Journal of Law and Technology*, vol. 7. pp. 103-120.
85. Singh Prakash, Terrorism and the Rule of Law. In N.R. Madhava Menon (Ed.), *Rule of Law in a Free Society*, (2008).
86. *Ibid.*
87. Foggetti, Nadina. (2010). Cyber Terrorism and The Right to Privacy in the Third Pillar Perspective, *Masaryk University Journal of Law and Technology*, Vol. 3: 3.
88. AIR 1990 SC 1962.

Chapter - 4

Women and Terrorism

Introduction

Terrorism is a deadly act of violence which has been on the rise around the world in the last few decades. The attack of September 11 2001, on the United States, demonstrated that worldwide terrorist organisations are operating with increasing complexity, audacity and lethality. Moreover, the possibility of a nuclear, biological and chemical attack has added a perilous new head to the terrorist hydra.

The evil of terrorism is not new. It is as old as the civilisation itself. It has merely adopted new shapes and forms in keeping with the times. The causes have also evolved over the years, as old problems are solved and new ones created. Moreover, it has gone hi-tech, like everything else. Its traces could be found in ancient Greece by the writings of Xenophon; during the rule of Roman Emperors in the first century A.D; the assassins; the Sircaris were all parts of a chain of terrorists historically.[1]

The genesis of modern terrorism took place during the French Revolution and the reaction that followed it; the state-sponsored terrorism executed some 40,000 people. The formation of terrorist outfit Ku Klux Klan after the American Civil War, the Anarchist Movement in Western Europe, Russia and the United States in the latter half of the 19th century gave credence to these activities. In the 20th century, terrorist attacks were carried out as far as India, Japan, and the Ottoman Empire and terrorism had become the hallmark of several political movements stretching from the extreme right to the extreme left of the political spectrum. Moreover, in the 21st century, the practice of terrorism becomes hi-tech. Since the last few decades, the world has been witnessing large scale violence has now become the order of the day both at the national and international level. Millions of people have lost their homes, lives, properties due to the evil of terrorism. It has spoiled the very nature of society and human beings.[2]

At first, glance, identifying the social and political conditions from which terrorist's campaigns emerge seems straight forward enough. Virtually everyone with an opinion on the subject knows that poverty and economic deprivation are the breeding grounds for terrorism. (If you drain the swamp, the mosquitoes will disappear; that is, if the government and international agencies promote economic development, providing with the hope for the future, terrorism will go away). Likewise, terrorism is encouraged by the absence of democracy. In countries where citizens are denied the right to participate peacefully in a political process, they naturally turn to political violence. If all channels of open political expression are blocked, aggrieved individuals will turn to terrorism as the only means available to make themselves heard. Promote freedom, and you will reduce or eliminate terrorism.[3]

The menace of terrorism is growing at large scale and affecting each and every individual irrespective of its nationality, religion, culture, ethnicity, etc., and becoming more dangerous in nature and impact. By the advancement in technology, terrorists too updated themselves. They are now eyeing on weapons of mass destruction and cyber technology though till now there has been no large scale destruction. However, apprehension is there if not checked, they will certainly going to explore new technologies in their favour. Then the most worrying fact is that now women are participating and playing a significant role in enhancing terrorist activities.

Women have played a less significant role in terrorist violence. Several mass-media sources as well as social-control sources, primarily the Federal Bureau of Investigation (FBI) and the International Association of Chiefs of Police (IACP) concluded that women had played a relatively secondary role in terrorist violence, as well as in terrorist groups in the past.[4] However, now conditions are favourable for their greater involvement in terrorist activities as freelance non-movement-oriented terrorists[5] as well as members of the terrorist organisation. Over the last decade, women have participated in over thirty-eight non-international armed conflicts as well as violent international disputes.[6] The countries that have experienced women in terrorist or militant organisations include Afghanistan, Angola, Burundi, Colombia, El Salvador, Ethiopia, Iraq, Guatemala, Eritrea, Lebanon, Liberia, Macedonia, Nepal, Peru, Sierra Leone, Sri Lanka, India and many others.[7]

Earlier women have not been involved in all types of terrorist activities. However, the roles of women in terrorist organisation were confined only to intelligence collection, operations as couriers, duties as nurses and medical personnel, and in the maintenance of safe houses for terrorists sought by police and for storage weapons, propaganda, false documentation, funds, and other supplies. For example, the elusive Venezuelan terrorist "Carlos," an individual associated with Popular Front for the Liberation of Palestine operations in Europe, used female contacts in Paris almost solely for the above-stated purposes.[8] However, at present times, female terrorism is visible and threatening event which cannot be brushed off or overlooked as it is used in the past years.[9] The future menace, that is, female terrorism, should be given proper consideration as women who have been identified as a mother of peace are now transforming themselves as destroyer of life.

Women and Terrorist Organisation

Although women have historically been participated in terrorist groups in Sri Lanka, Iran, West Germany and Japan, to name a few cases, very little scholarly attention has been paid to this mode of terrorism.[10] Generally, most terrorist are male many terrorism specialists have noted that the number of women involved in terrorism has dramatically surpassed the number of women involved in ordinary crime.[11] Since 1985 to 2006, over 220 female suicide attacks occurred this constitutes approximately 15% of the total suicide attacks worldwide.[12] Some female terrorist has created immense climate of fear, and, females carried on long term, low-level conflict at a deadly rate in various countries at different times. Female terrorist take roles similar to those held by women in revolutionary organisations from earliest times. For example, in 2007, there were eight instances of a female suicide bombing in Iraq. As of August 2008, 27 female suicide bombers gave their lives in support of the insurgency.[13]

One of the earliest recorded incidents of women involved in terrorism was the assassination of Tsar Alexander II of Russia in 1881. Sophia Perovskaya was a member of the executive committee of the Narodnaya Volya or the People's Will. Ten of the first twenty-nine members of the executive committee were females, and eleven terrorists attacks were conducted by women from 1905 to 1909.[14] According to Knight in the 1905 Revolution in Russia, Women showed absolute devotion to violence and a strong tendency towards extremism. He pointed out that "Several became fanatics, seeing the terror and their heroic self-sacrifice as an end in itself. The ultimate test and devotion to the revolution was their willingness to die."[15]

In the modern era, a significant number of women voluntary choose to die for their revolutionary ideals, and they have been considered peripheral players by both observers and many terrorist organisations. Women have been held in a vital position in some organisation, for instance, Shigenobu Fusako, founder and leader of the Japanese Red Army (JRA) and Ulrike Meinhof. Further, women largely dominated the substantial number of the West Germany Baader–Meinhof Gang and this leftist terrorist organisation.[16]Ulrike Meinhof and Gudrun Ensslin, the famous member of Baader-Meinhof gang, even left their children behind when they went underground, this shows that they transformed their behaviour contrary to motherhood, peacefulness and maternal ethic.[17] In Iran, Ashraf Rabi was arrested in 1974 by the SAVAK, the country's secret police, after a bomb accidentally detonated in her headquarters.[18] Apart from these organisations, women also hold an essential position in Sri Lanka's Tamil Tigers, Germany Red Army Faction, Italy's Red Brigade, Spain Basque (ETA) and the Japanese Red Army. In Sri Lanka, women have been effective suicide bombers for Liberation Tigers for the Tamil Elam (LTTE), and interestingly, their role is modelled after women participation in the Indian National Army (INA) during the 1940's war with Britain, which included female suicide bombers.[19]

The Kurdish and Tamil terrorist groups have been using women as suicide terrorists for many years, but this was unnoticed in the west.

Generally, speaking women are underrepresented in many terrorist groups, but they are over-represented among PKK and LTTE suicide terrorists.[20] In recent years women have been very much in evidence among Chechen suicide terrorists. The Black Widows are a female terrorist organisation that provided help in the struggle for Chechen independence. The organisation developed its exclusive costume to differentiate themselves from orthodox Chechen insurgents.[21] The organisation gained widespread international attention after being significantly involved in the two most significant hostage incidents associated with suicide terrorism. On October 23–26 Chechen terrorists seized 700 hostages in a Dubrovka Theatre Moscow. The episode ended with the deaths of scores of hostages and all of the terrorists. As per the reports of the Russian authorities, many of the hostage-takers were women who had suicide explosive vests strapped to their bodies.[22] In September 2004, two females took part in hostage-taking of the Beslan School in North Ossetia along with terrorists male terrorists.[23]The Russian media has dubbed the women Chechen terrorist as 'Black Widow' as they are allegedly relatives of Chechen men who have died in the ongoing war.[24] On June 7, 2000, Khava Barayeva and Luisa Magomadova became known as the first "Black Widows" after they drove a truck into headquarters of a Russian Special Forces detachment in the village of Alkan Yurt in Chechnya.[25] The reasons for the motivation of the Black widows are not easy to ascertain; however, the critical reason behind Chechen female terrorism has been enormous wrath, resentment and animosity against Russian. Chechen female terrorists were influenced by conflict zones of trauma, revenge, nationalism and expression of community outrage. They were not forced to join suicide terrorism; they volunteered willingly.[26] It was claimed that Chechens had employed a considerable number of women than any other Islamic-related terror groups; [27]it is estimated that "42 per cent of Chechen suicide bombers have been women.[28] It was also asserted that these Chechen women were religiously influenced by Wahhabist violent credo and were attempting to become martyrs, assuming that they would be reunited with loved ones in heaven. However, it was only when Palestinian groups began to use women; the western nations began to pay attention pay and were terrified.

According to Russell and Miller, women played a more prominent role in the left-wing terrorism in the year 1966–76 periods than in violent crime in general. Russell and Miller's data reveals that the large numbers of terrorist were male and played the primary role. The women were comparably less in number played a secondary support role in most of the organisations, particularly, the Uruguayan Tupamaros and several European groups. For instance, they point out that women constituted one-third of the personnel of the RAF and June Second Movement, and that nearly 60 per cent of the RAF and June Second Movement who were at large in August 1976 were women. They further pointed out that "urban terrorism remains a predominantly male phenomenon," with women functioning mainly in a secondary support role, may underestimate the active, operational role played by women in Latin American and West European terrorist organisations in the 1970 and 1980s. Insurgents groups in Latin America in the 1970's and 1980 reportedly included large percentages of female combatants: thirty per cent of the Sandinista National Liberation Front (FSLN) combatants in Nicaragua by the late 1970's; one-third of the combined forces of the Farabundo Marti National Liberation Front (FMLN) in El Salvador; and one half of the Shining Path terrorist in Peru.[29] Even the right-wing extremist groups in the United States, such as the World Church of the Creator (WCOTC) are reportedly witnessing high female recruitment levels and one women associated with the rightist movement, Erica Chase, went on trial in summer 2002 with her boyfriend in an alleged plot to bomb symbolic African–American and Jewish Targets.[30]

The Liberation Tigers of Tamil Eelam (LTTE) is a terrorist organisation which also recruited women to perform terrorist acts to achieve their objectives. In LTTE presence of women cadres in Black Tigers is a distinct phenomenon. The Vituthalia Pulikal Makalir Munani (Women's Front of the Liberations Tigers) was formed in 1983 and performed various roles, including propaganda work, the provision of medical care, fundraising, and as combatants.[31] The first group of Women Tigers had their training in Tamil Nadu camps by 1985 and had their first taste of combat in July 1986. It is also claimed that the Popular Front substantially inspired the LTTE for the Liberation of Palestine; both organisations were indoctrinated in Lebanon in 1977 and 1984. It was also asserted that Leila Khalid's manoeuvres motivated the LTTE's determination to recruit women.[32] In October 1987, the

LTTE leader Vellupillai Prabhakaran set up a training camp exclusively for women in Jaffna for the second and successive batches.[33] By 1989, this unit secured its leadership structure. In the same year, women were recruited for the Sea Tigers, which was then in a growing stage. As in the case of selecting males for Black Tiger operations, the LTTE central military command selects, instead accepts, volunteer women for suicidal mission.[34] Women also have to go rigorous training as the male members, they ride bicycles, drive motor vehicles, swimming and seafaring that gives them a sense of empowerment, confidence and equality.[35] It has been documented that the LTTE has "orchestrated more suicide attacks with women than any other terrorist organisation worldwide."[36] Jane's Intelligence Review states that "from 1980 to 200, the LTTE performed 168 suicide attacks about 30 per cent used women cadres."[37] Women terrorists in the LTTE killed and injured thousands and cost the Government of Sri Lanka and private businesses millions of dollars in damages.[38]The most worthy of attention suicide bombing executed by a woman in the LTTE was the assassination of the former Prime Minister of India in 1991. Females in the LTTE participated at all levels within the organisation.

For several decades Palestinians also have included women in suicide as part of their arsenal. Palestinian women were given supportive and passive responsibility in a Palestinian liberation terrorist group.[39] This situation became even more sensitive and aggravated when the High Islamic Council in Saudi Arabia issued a fatwa or edict, which decreed that women should join men as suicide martyrs for Islam.[40] Leila Khalid, a beautiful PFLP commando was one of the female terrorists of modern international terrorism; she probably inspired hundreds of other angry young women around the world.[41] In 1969, Leila was part of a team that hijacked TWA flight 840 and diverted it to Damascus where all one hundred and thirteen passengers were released unharmed. Although her identity was revealed to the world by the Syrians, Leila continued her terrorism career. In September 1970, Leila and Patrick Arguello, a Nicaraguan attempted the hijack of El Al Flight 219 but was detained in London by British Police. Before the hijacking of El Al Flight, she underwent at least three secret plastic surgery operations to escape herself from getting arrested.[42] Wafa Idris, the member of Al Aqsa Martyrs Brigade, was the first female suicide bomber in the Israeli-Palestinian conflict. Ayat Akhras, another member of the Al Aqsa Martyrs Brigade, blew herself up outside a Jerusalem supermarket on March 3, 2002. Ayat stated that she was going to fight instead of sleeping with Arab armies who were watching Palestinian girls fighting alone until victory.[43]

Over a year later the ever – manipulative President of the Palestinian Authority decided to try another twist and exploit one of the advantages of the secular groups, their female supporters. In January 2002 Arafat addressed a crowd of over a thousand Palestinian women. He pronounced them to be the equal of men and declared: "You are my army of roses that will crush Israeli Tanks." In this speech he coined the feminine form of the word 'Shaheed', chanting 'Shahida, Shahida, until Jerusalem.'[44] The rapid development in information technology and communication brought the propaganda effect of female terrorism and increased the support of the Palestinian female terrorists.

Islamic Fundamentalists have a view of women as property to be protected that would appear to be incompatible with their playing the role of soldiers, much less martyrs. al-Qaeda, for example, have not deployed women on a suicide mission at the initial stage, although in late 2005 al – Qaeda and its affiliated organisations appeared to be willing to do so. There were eight female suicide bombers in the year 2007 with multiplication in the following year to twenty-seven by the middle of August.[45] al-Qaeda has managed females to carry out several suicide acts; for instance, Muriel Degauque blew herself up near a U.S. Army patrol in Mosul. These female attacks show that women are zealously participating in terrorism in Iraq, and al- Qaeda is relying on them as assets to their organisation.[46] The experience of women against Israel appears to be a consequence of the rivalry between religious and secular groups battling for the role of legislative representative of the Palestinian people.[47]

The secular groups were not the only ones to respond to sentiments. Initially, Sheikh Ahmed Yassin, the spiritual leader of Hamas, declared that any man who recruits women to be a martyr is breaking Islamic Law. He viewed that 'He is taking the girl or woman without the permission of her father, brother or husband. Therefore the family of a girl confronts an even greater problem since the man has the biggest power over her choosing the day that she will give her life back to Allah.' With time, Hamas changed its tune. Yassin later said that 'The Prophet always emphasised the woman's rights to wage jihad.'[48]

Reasons and Motivation to Join Terrorist Organisation

There are numerous grounds responsible for persons to become terrorists such as the social and political conditions, poverty and economic deprivation, likewise, terrorism is encouraged by the absence of democracy, and at the same time causes can be found in the religion and globalisation.[49] The reasons for why women participate in acts of terrorism are not widely researched. There have been mainly two aspects of being a female terrorist. One by participating in terrorist activities they have been gaining honour and respect. The other possible dimension may be that in the terrorist organisation they are humiliated and subjugated, and are forced to become suicide bombers.[50] Trapped in traditional culture, family tyranny and grinding gender inequality, young women began to come out from home not only for ethnic liberation but also for their empowerment as well. They have equal status alongside men in the organisation, something they could never have enjoyed at another place or time. They undergo the same political and military training. This sense of equality reinforced by a strong sense of duty that is larger than life seems to be conducive to scarifying a life that had little meaning before. Within LTTE was the specialised 'Women's Front of the Liberation Tigers', founded in 1983. The five main objectives of the Women's front's front, also known as the 'Birds of Freedom' were as follows (1) to secure the right to self-determination of the Tamil people and establish an independent democratic state of Tamil Eelam. (2) to abolish the oppressive caste discrimination and semi-feudal customs. (3) to eliminate all discrimination against Tamil women to secure social, political and economic equality. (4) to ensure control over their own lives, and (5) finally to ensure legal protection for women against sexual violence.[51] Vellupillai Prabhakaran, the leader of the LLTE, spoke out about women's involvement in the armed struggle. International Women's Day was also celebrated as Tamil Eelam Women's Day, and three different times (1992, 1993 and 1996) Prabhakaran delivered speeches expressing his views on the role of women.[52] In the year 1992, he spoke about the oppression of women as a social injustice occurring in all cultures worldwide. Tamil women specifically, 'subject to intolerable suffering as a consequence of male chauvinistic oppression, violence and form of the social evils of casteism and dowry' and that their 'awakening is crucial' in order them to 'rebel and re-orient their wretched conditions of existence' in order for their true emancipation. In these circumstances mentioned above, the loyalty of women to the organisation and its leader might well have been even stronger than that of the men. Moreover, the supportive role of women is not the product of male chauvinism but rather practical experience. In the minds of the most terrorist leaders, and as demonstrated by actual operations, women are more effective than men in such supportive activities.[53] Moreover, the increasing role of women in such activities may be due to shortage of men within the organisation caused by personnel being captured, killed, or unwilling to participate.[54]

There are other certain reasons which are advantageous for the leaders of the terrorists' groups to recruit women. Female arouse less suspicion from the security forces. They can be equipped with explosives and dresses as though they are pregnant making likely to frisk them as they approach the target.[55] Female terrorists can use their gender stereotypes to avoid detection as their 'non-threatening nature may prevent in-depth scrutiny'; they are not perceived as able to be guilty of terrorist acts.[56] Some instances of how females have used their gender specifically to commit a terrorist act include a suicide bomber appearing to be pregnant in order to gain entrance to a hospital, successfully killing and injuring numerous people including the commander of the Sri Lankan Army. Similarly, a woman assassinated the Indian prime minister in 1991 after offering him a garland of flowers.[57] Women can perform cooking, sewing and other household chores for the revolution and also may be available for the sex. At the same time, they can provide access to resources and the ability to carry on a clandestine life amid warfare. Their participation in the terrorist campaign is less direct and of necessity and are not usually identified publicly with the group.[58] Women can also act as warriors, using weapons and incendiary devices. They can fight in the battle on an equal status with men.[59] In other words, terrorists' organisation provides an opportunity for upward mobility, in leadership and in an active role in formulating the group's policies, opportunities that are absent or extremely limited in the male-dominated society of legitimate activity.[60] The increasing role of women in terrorist organisation in many cases can be attributed to meet a need or a shortage within the organisation. Terrorist organisations are struggling with a shortage of available personnel as the number of male member being captured, killed, or unwilling to support the cause.[61]Use of female terrorism also produces tactical advantages, since they can be useful in the roles of decoys, messengers, intelligence gathers, and spies.[62] Moreover, women can also inspire other members of the groups.[63]

What motivates women to become a terrorist? Interviews with the family members and friends of the first female Palestinian suicide bombers suggested that the motives of these women might be somewhat different from those of their male counterparts.[64] Gavin argues that women terrorist enters into terrorism with different motivations and expectations than male terrorist.[65] Behind the usual rhetoric, these female trailblazers were also fighting powerful personal demons. Her husband had divorced Wafa Idris because of her failure to produce a child, and she had been forced to return to her fatherless family. Her child was stillborn, bringing shame to herself and her family. A month later, Darine Abu Aisha followed in her footsteps. This twenty-one year old, university student was profoundly depressed and under intense pressure from her family. She had been forced by Israeli guards to kiss a male cousin in public, which had deeply shamed her.[66] In other words, personal tragedy or revenge is one of the most significant motivations for women to join and support a terrorist organisation.

With the increase in the number of female martyrs, the motivating factors also changed. Promises of power and glory attract them. Andalib Suleiman was motivated by a desire to become a superstar. She was fascinated by the celebrity of martyrs and replaced the pop–star posters on her bedroom walls with those of martyrs. She also wanted the assurance that after she died, she would be famous all over the Arab world.[67] Companionship is another motivating factor in woman's joining a terrorist group. Susanna Ronconi and Ulrike Meinhof "craved love, comradeship, and emotional support" from their comrades.[68]

Conclusion

Women comprise a self-conscious, dynamic sector of our society which often perceives itself to be an oppressed majority. Women from every corner of the world irrespective of their caste, creed, religion and community face discrimination. At the international as well as at the national level, women are struggling to break the shackles that bind them by fighting against the unequal distribution of power in the society. However, the women and men enjoy a different status in society; it is humanmade; nature has very little to do with it. It is gender, not sex which has determined that (almost) everywhere, women as a group are considered inferior to men. They face systemic violence at the hands of men and society; and they have little decision – making power in social, economic, and political institutions.[69] They are living a frustrated life, and in order to find some status and equality and to take revenge, they join the terrorist organisation. The fact that women have been and will continue to serve in terrorist groups, whether right-wing, left-wing or religious is disastrous for the society. Moreover, as terrorist organisations are very well aware of their potential, they attract women to join their organisations and provide them the equal status with that of male terrorists which gives them a sense of equality and empowerment. Furthermore, till the society will show disrespect towards women, will not treat them equally, will not empower them, will not make them economically self-sufficient they will keep on joining such terrorist organisations and which is not suitable for the health of the society; and the menace of terrorism will keep on destructing the peace across the world and no draconian or soft law can stop terrorism activities from the world.

Notes

1. Ujjwal Kumar Singh, *The State, Democracy and Anti Terror Laws in India*, (2007), at 305.
2. Maj. Gen. R S Mehta (ed.), *International Encyclopaedia of Terrorism Laws*, (2007), at 866.
3. K.G. Kannabiran, "The State as a Terrorist", *Express Magazine*, dated June 23, 1985.
4. See Daniel E. Georges-Abeyie, "Women as Terrorist", in *Perspective on Terrorism*, Lawrence Zelic Freedman & Yonah Alexander (ed), (1985).
5. Individuals who commit terrorist acts, yet are not the members of the organization.

6. See, Jordon, K and Denov, M., (2007), "Birds of Freedom? Perspectives on Female Emancipation and Srilanka's Liberation Tigers of Tamil Eelam," *Journal of International Women's Studies* 9(1), 42.
7. *Ibid.*
8. See, "The Number 1 Terrorist," *Japan Times Weekly* (Tokyo), 4 March 1975 and *Informaciones* (Madrid), 11 July 1975, pp. 2-3, articles entitled, "Carlos, el terrorista es miembro de FPLP" and "La embajada cubana en Paris, complicada en el terrorismo," and the three-part series in *Der Spiegel*, 26 July, 2 and 9 August 1976, as cited in (Delhi, Hindustan Publishing Corporation, 1985).
9. See O'Connor, A.S. (2007a), Picked Last Women and Terrorism, *Joint Force Quarterly*, 44, 95-100.
10. Karla J. Cunningham, "Cross-Regional Trends in Female Terrorism", *The New Era of Terrorism: A Selected Readings*, Gus Martin (ed.), (2004), p. 90.
11. Rex A. Hudson, The Sociology and Psychology of Terrorism: Who Becomes a Terrorist and Why?, A Report Prepared under an Interagency Agreement by the Federal Research Division, Library of Congress, September 1999, p. 33, at http://www.loc.gov/rr/frd/, accessed on 24 April 2006.
12. Mia Bloom, *Women as Victims and Victimizers*, (April 11, 2008), http://www.america.gov/st/peacesec-english/2008/April/20080522172353SrenoD016383936.html (accessed on September 15, 2014).
13. See Steve Niva, "Behind the Surge in Iraqui Women Suicide Bombers," *Foreign Policy in Focus*, (August 11, 2008), http://www.fpif.org/fpiftxt/5455 (accessed on September 15 2014).
14. Amy Knight, "Female Terrorists in the Russian Socialist Revolutionary Party", *Russian Review* 38 (1979): 139.
15. Pamala L Griset, Sue Mahan, *Terrorism in Perspective*, (2003), p. 157.
16. Rex A. Hudson, The Sociology and Psychology of Terrorism: Who Becomes a Terrorist and Why?, A Report Prepared under an Interagency Agreement by the Federal Research Division, Library of Congress, September 1999, p. 53, at http://www.loc.gov/rr/frd/, accessed on 24 April 2006.
17. Melzer, P. (2011) Maternal Ethics and Political Violence: The Betrayal of Motherhood among the women of the RAF and June 2 Movement. *Seminar 47.1, A Journal of Politics, 10(3)*, 282-298.
18. Karla J. Cunningham, "Cross-Regional Trends in Female Terrorism", *The New Era of Terrorism: A Selected Readings,* Gus Martin (ed.), (2004), p. 91.
19. *Ibid.*
20. Louise Richardson, *What Terrorists Want: Understanding the Terrorist Threat*, (London, John Murray, 2006), p. 152.
21. Ryan Chilcote, "Russia's Balck Widows' Wreak Terror," CNN, (September 3, 2004), http://edition.cnn.com/2004/WORLD/europe/09/01/russia.widows/index.html. (Accessed on May 17, 2009)
22. Anne Speckard and Khapta Akhmedova, "Black Widows and Beyond" in *Female Terrorism and Militancy: Agency, Utility and Organisation*, by Cindy D. Ness (Newyork, Ny Routledge, 2008).
23. *Ibid.*

24. Gus Martin, *Understanding Terrorism: Challenges, Perspectives, and Issues*, (2006), p.99. See also, See O'Connor, A.S. (2007a), Picked Last Women and Terrorism, *Joint Force Quarterly*, 44, 95-100. See, Jane's Intelligenence Digest, *Deadlier Than the Male?* Briefing , (Surrey, U.K.: Jane's Information Group, 2003).
25. Anne Speckard and Khapta Akhmedova, "Black Widows and Beyond" in *Female Terrorism and Militancy: Agency, Utility and Organisation*, by Cindy D. Ness (Newyork, Ny Routledge, 2008).
26 See Speckhard, A. "Terrorists are made not born: Creating Terrorists using Social Psychological Conditioning, Accessed on 12 October 2014 at http://www.homelandsecurity.org/journal/articles/stahelski.html.
27. *Ibid.*
28. Anne Speckard and Khapta Akhmedova, "Black Widows and Beyond" in *Female Terrorism and Militancy: Agency, Utility and Organisation*, by Cindy D. Ness (Newyork, Ny Routledge, 2008).
29. Rex A. Hudson, *The Sociology and Psychology of Terrorism: Who Becomes a Terrorist and Why?*, A Report Prepared under an Interagency Agreement by the Federal Research Division, Library of Congress, September 1999, p. 53, at http://www.loc.gov/rr/frd/, accessed on 24 April 2006.
30. Karla J. Cunningham, "Cross-Regional Trends in Female Terrorism", in *The New Era of Terrorism: A Selected Readings*, Gus Martin (ed.), (2004), p. 91.
31. Jordon Kim, Myriam Denov,"Birds of Freedom? Perspectives on Female Emancipation and Sri Lanka's Lberation Tigers of tamil Eelam", *Journal of International Women's* Studies 9no. 1 (Novenber 2007), 46.
32. See O'Connor, A.S. (2007a), Picked Last Women and Terrorism, *Joint Force Quarterly*, 44-48.
33. See, Battacharji, P, (2009), Backgrounder: Liberation Tigers of Tamil Eelam (aka Tamil Tigers) (Sri Lanka, saparatists), Council on Foreign Relations, http://www.cfr.org/separatist-terrorism/liberation-tigers-tamil-eelam-aka-tamil-tigers-sri-lanka-separatists/p9242#p3 Accesses on 21 September 2014.
34. Liberation Tigers of Tamil Eelam, Institute of Conflict Management, http://www.satp.org/satporg/countries/ShrilLanka/terroristoutfits/Ltte.htm. Accessed on 24 September 2005.
35. See, Alison, M, (2003), Cogs in the Wheel? Women in the Liberation Tigers of Tmail Eelam, *Civil Wars*, 6(4), 37-54.
36. Jordon Kim, Myriam Denov,"Birds of Freedom? Perspectives on Female Emancipation and Sri Lanka's Lberation Tigers of tamil Eelam", *Journal of International Women's* Studies 9no. 1 (November 2007), 46
37. Siddharth Srivastava, "Women terrorists on the Rise in India", *New America Media*, (October 2, 2003), http://news.pacificnews.org/news/view_article_id=3eeea82ae0d4741ec00d163d72d259bda, (Accessed on June 10, 2008)
38. See, Mahan Sue, Pamela L. Griset, *Terrorism in Perspective*, (Thousand Oaks, CA: Sage Publication, 2008)
39. Cagla Gul Yesevi, "Female Terrorism", *European Scientific Journal*, Vol. 10 No. 14, at 583. See, Berko, A. and Erez, E. (2007). Gender, Palestinian Women,

and Terrorism: Women's Liberation or Oppression. *Studies in Conflict and Terrorism,* 30(6), 493-519.

40. Pamala L. Griset and Sue Mahan, *Terrorism in Perspective*, (2003), p. 158.
41. See, Ness, C.D. (2008). "In the Name of the Cause: Women's Work in Secular and Religious terrorism", *Conflict &* terrorism" 28(5), 353-373. See also Rex A. Hudson, The Sociology and Psychology of Terrorism: Who Becomes a Terrorist and Why?, A Report Prepared under an Interagency Agreement by the Federal Research Division, Library of Congress, September 1999, p. 74, at http://www.loc.gov/rr/frd/, accessed on 24 April 2006.
42. Cagla Gul Yesevi, "Female Terrorism", *European Scientific Journal*, Vol. 10 No.14, at 583. See, Berko, A. and Erez, E. (2007). Gender, Palestinian Women, and Terrorism: Women's Liberation or Oppression. *Studies in Conflict and Terrorism,* 30(6), 493-519. See also, Rex A. Hudson, The Sociology and Psychology of Terrorism: Who Becomes a Terrorist and Why?, A Report Prepared under an Interagency Agreement by the Federal Research Division, Library of Congress, September 1999, p. 74, at http://www.loc.gov/rr/frd/, accessed on 24 April 2006. See also, Debra D. Zedalis, "Beyond the Bombings: Analyzing Female Suicide Bombers," in *Female Terrorism and Militancy: Agency, Utility and Organisation*, by Cindy D. Ness, (New York, NY: Routledge, 2008).
43. See, O'Connor, A.S. "Picked Last Women and Terrorism", *Joint Force Quarterly*, (2007a), 44, 95-100.
44. Louise Richardson, What Terrorists Want: Understanding the Terrorist Threat, (2006), p.153. See alao, Paige Whaley Eager, *From Freedom Fighter to Terrorists: Women and Political Violence*, (Burlington, VT: Ashgate Publishing Group, 2008).
45. Niva Steve, "Behind the Surge in Iraqi Women Suicide Bombers." Foreign Policy in Focus, August 11, 2008, http://www.fpif.org/fpiftxt/5455. (accessed on September 4, 2008).
46. Christopher Dickey, "Terror: Women of Al Qaeda," *Newsweek International Edition*, (December 12, 2005): 27.
47. Louise Richardson, What Terrorists Want: Understanding the Terrorist Threat, (2006), p. 152.
48. *Ibid.*
49. See, Post, J.M., Sprinzak, E, Denny, M.D. (2003), 'The Terrorists in Their Own Words: Interviews with 35 Incarcerated Middle Eastern Terrorists'. *Terrorism and Political Violence*, 15(1), 171-184.
50. Cagla Gul Yesevi, 'Female terrorism', *European Scientific Journal*, vol. 10. No.14, 580.
51. Schalk, P, 1996, Women Fighters of the Liberation Tigers in Tamil Ilam, *South Asia Research*, 14(2), 163-195. See also O'Connor, A.S. (2007a), Picked Last Women and Terrorism, *Joint Force Quarterly*, 95-100.
52. See Mehta, R.K, , *Lost Victory: The Rise & Fall of LTTE Supremo, V. Prabhakaran*, (New Delhi Pentagon Security International 2010)
53. See, Fox, MJ, (2006), Girl Soldiers: Human Security and Gendered Insecurity, *Security Dialogue*, 35(4). 465-479.

54. See, Cunningham, K, (2003), Cross-Regional Trends in Female Terrorism, *studies in Conflict & Terrorism*, 26:171-195, 2003.See also, Sutten, M, (2009), The Rising Importance of Women in Terrorism and the Need to Reform Counterterrorism Strategy, United States Army, Monograph, www.dtic.mil/cgi-bin/GetTRDoc?AD=ADA506225.
55. *Ibid.*
56. Prof. Dogu Ergil, "Suicide Terrorism in Turkey: The Case of the Worker's Party of Kurdistan, *Countering Suicide Terrorism*, International Institute of Counter-Terrorism (ICT), 2000, p.83-84. See also, Cunningham, K, (2003), Cross-Regional Trends in Female Terrorism, *studies in Conflict & Terrorism*, 26:171-195, 2003.See also, Sutten, M, (2009), The Rising Importance of Women in Terrorism and the Need to Reform Counterterrorism Strategy, United States Army, Monograph, www.dtic.mil/cgi-bin/GetTRDoc?AD=ADA506225.
57. Melissa Martin, 'Women's Participation in Terrorism, Conflict and Violent Extremism: Gender Equality or Pure Pragmatism?, at http://www.nottingham.ac.uk/hrlc/documents/student-conference-2014/m-martin-ms-nottinghamstudentconference.pdf (Accessed on 25 September 2014).
58. Pamala L. Griset and Sue Mahan, *Terrorism in Perspective*, (2003), p. 159.
59. *Ibid.*
60. See, Daniel E. Georges-Abeyie, "Women as Terrorist", in *Perspective on Terrorism*, Lawrence Zelic Freedman & Yonah Alexander (ed), (Delhi, Hindustan Publishing Corporation, 1985).
61. Alisa Stack-o'Conner, "Picked Last: Womenin Terrorism," *Joint Forces Quarterly*, 44, 1st Quarter (2008), 98.
62. Pamala L. Griset and Sue Mahan, Terrorism in Perspective, (2003), p. 159.
63. *Ibid.*
64. Louise Richardson, What Terrorists Want: Understanding the Terrorist Threat, (2006), p. 155.
65. Rex A. Hudson, The Sociology and Psychology of Terrorism: Who Becomes a Terrorist and Why?, A Report Prepared under an Interagency Agreement by the Federal Research Division, Library of Congress, September 1999, p. 58, at http://www.loc.gov/rr/frd/, accessed on 24 April 2006.
66. Louise Richardson, What Terrorists Want: Understanding the Terrorist Threat, (2006), p.155.
67. *Ibid.*
68. Rex A. Hudson, The Sociology and Psychology of Terrorism: Who Becomes a Terrorist and Why?, A Report Prepared under an Interagency Agreement by the Federal Research Division, Library of Congress, September 1999, p. 59, at http://www.loc.gov/rr/frd/, accessed on 24 April 2006.
69. *Ibid.*

Chapter - 5

Terrorism and Weapon of Mass Destruction

Killing, hijackings, abductions, and bombings are still the first and most favourite choice of terrorists. The estrapade on World Trade Centre and Pentagon on September 11 showed that these traditional methods could be employed to inflict painful destruction. In the present, the threat posed by the contemporary terrorist is more horrific and devastating because of the fact that the weapon of mass destructions are within their reach. Today, they have the opportunity to possess and use the most lethal weapons on the earth (Nuclear weapon, Biological weapon and Chemical Weapon) and can destruct any area of the earth and can cause millions of deaths and injuries. These weapons could create global terror and dismantle the government's effort to fight the terror.

The supposition that life on earth will come to a violent end is ancient and has often been imagined as a consequence of some giant conflagration, a flood, collision with a comet, or some mysterious plague. The supernatural power was made responsible, either out of caprice or wrath with what humankind had wrought. However, the supposition of human beings has crafted the characters of mad scientist (or mere technician) capable of sabotaging entire cities, continents, and even planet.[1]

The fiction, in which some scientist who was the powerhouse of knowledge indulged themselves in harmful and destructive application of their knowledge and like mad man deliberately tried to bring about the end of the life on earth, became a subgenre of literature, widely read and quite influential. Moreover, no scientist in that age of great scientific achievement came forward to criticise these fiction stories, however, few scientists, such as the French astronomer, even made notable contributions to such pieces of literature. What was once read in the fictitious book is now becoming a reality, due to the easy availability of raw material to manufacture the weapons of mass destruction, the imagination is now converted into reality.

The weapon of mass destruction is a former soviet military term which was euphemistically used to indicate nuclear, biological, and chemical weapons (NBC), or atomic, biological, and chemical weapons (ABC).[2] The terrorists of the present era may strike with the central objective of killing as many people as possible. They are not necessarily interested in overthrowing governments or changing policies as their primary objectives. Instead, they intend to deliver a high body count and thereby terrorise and disrupt large audiences. For example, the 1993 and 2001 attacks on the World Trade Centre in New York city by radical Islamists, Aum Shinrikyo's 1995 sarin nerve gas attack in Tokyo, and the 1995 bombing in Oklahoma City by American terrorists were all intended to kill as many civilians as possible and to demonstrate the vulnerability of society.[3]

Advances and progress mould the terrorist environment in the present modern period, such as technology, information, and transnational connectivity. This truly globalised environment has given rise to new possibilities in terrorist methodologies. Two factors, in particular, are believed by experts to contribute significantly to the distinctiveness in the way of working in the present modern era.[4]

The first is "the diffusion of information technology and advanced communications." The anxiety concerning the use of WMD by terrorists emanates from the fact the information relating to creation and use of such weapons is readily available on the internet. The significant impact of the new electronic technologies, however, has not been to move the terrorists towards more exotic methods of attack, but rather to improve the efficiency of all their activities. New technologies such as computers and satellite phones have become standard equipment in terrorist groups.[5]

A second distinctive factor is the "increased movement, and ease of movement, across international boundaries." The terrorists' more exceptional ability to operate over long distances has manifested itself in the building by several terrorist groups of global - circling infrastructure (and) the rise of ad hoc terrorists - small cabals of extremists who do not belong to any more significant, established, previously known group.[6]

In the past, terrorism was practised by a collection of individuals belonging to an identifiable organisation with a specific ideology and superior head. They had specific economic, political and social agenda. For example, Radical leftist (i.e., Marxist-Leninist/ Maoist/ Stalinist movements) organisations, the Japanese Red Army, the Red Army Faction in Germany, the Red Brigades in Italy *inter alia,* as well as ethno-nationalist terrorist movements like the PLO, Palestinian splinter group like the Abu Nidal Organisation. They usually distributed messages taking credit for and explaining in great detail- the actions and however, their belief and motives were at least apparent albeit politically radical and personally fanatical.[7]

The terrorist groups were engaged in extremely selective and often discriminated acts of violence. Their violence was cautiously designed in such a way to invoke their real or imaginary constituents and thus kept within the parameters of what the terrorists' believed their constituency deemed "acceptable." Terrorists, therefore, were seen as being careful not to undertake action that might alienate their supports and sympathisers. It seems that they were acquainted of the likelihood that acts of mass destruction or bloodshed might result not only in public revulsion and alienation, but, it might trigger severe governmental reprisals or countermeasures as well.

For this reason, the violence used by the left-wing terrorists were mostly slenderly proscribed. Their self-styled crusade for social justice was often typically directed against governmental or commercial institutions or persons they believed represented capitalist exploitation and repression.[8]

The approach adopted by the ethno-nationalist and separatist groups of that era, such as PLO, IRA, and ETA, were similar to the left-wing terrorists. Although the acts of terrorism by ethno-nationalist and separatist groups were often more destructive and caused more casualties than those of their left-wing counterparts, the same self-imposed constraints and balancing act of finding a level of violence acceptable to their actual or perceived constituents was evident. In the broader sense, ethno-nationalist and separatist terrorism were also tailored to appeal to international as well as internal opinion in support of the terrorists' irredentist or nationalist aims. Therefore, to continue to receive the support of their constituency, to generate sympathy among the international community and, to forestall active governmental countermeasures as well, these terrorists exerted to regulate and confined their violence.[9]

Although the radical or revolutionary these groups were politically oriented, the vast majority were also equally conservative in their actions. Such terrorist organisations were more demonstrably "imitative than innovative" with a minimal tactical repertoire that was mostly directed against a similarly narrow target set.[10] The little innovation that was observed was in the mode of choosing the targets rather than devising new methodology for destructive violence.

In the present era, many traditional kinds of ethnic/nationalist and separatist as well as ideological group have joined by several other organisations with less- understandable nationalist or ideological motivations. These new terrorist organisations embrace for more amorphous religious and millenarian aims and wrap themselves in less-cohesive organisational entities, with a more-diffuse structure and membership. The appearance of these different types of adversaries with new motivations and different capabilities accounts mostly for terrorism's enhanced lethality in recent years.[11]

The terrorist groups such as Germany's RAF, Italy's Red Brigades, and some Palestinian organisations- admittedly had tried to experiment using such indiscriminately lethal weapons. However, none had ever tried practically to apply their heinous thought or executed their half-baked plots. For example, the RAF, Italy's Red Brigades and some Palestinian organisations had at one time, or the other 'recruited microbiologists purchased bacteriological experimentation equipment and dabbled in sending toxins such as anthrax to potential victims. In 1979 Palestinian terrorists were suspected of having poisoned some

Jaffa oranges which were exported to Europe to sabotage Israel's economy. Nearly a decade later small traces of cyanide were found in Chilean grapes exported to the United States by the left-wing Chilean group. However, together with a few other inconsequential incidents, this handful of inchoate or poorly conceived attempts was mostly the extent of actual terrorist use of such "non-conventional" weapons and tactics.[12]

Even when experts in 1970s thought about possible terrorist use of WMD, there was unanimity of thought among the world leaders that terrorists would axiomatically prefer nuclear or radiological weapons over chemical or biological ones.[13] Brian Jenkins observed that: "Terrorists imitate governments, and nuclear weapons are in the arsenal of the world's major powers. That makes them "legitimate." Chemical and biological armaments are found in the stores of many states. However, the use of such weapons has been sharply criticised by the people and proscribed by treaty, although in recent past the constraints against the use of such weapons seem to be eroding."[14]

However, more significantly, the observation made by Jenkins that "Terrorists want many people watching and many people listening, and not many people died,"[15] was generally accepted by one and all. In 1975, regarding the threat of terrorist use of radiological or nuclear weapons, Jenkins argued, "Circumstances concerning the measured diffusion of harmful radioactive material.... do not seem to suit the way the terrorist actions are carried out so far... Terrorist actions have inclined to generate instant intense effects, a handful of violent deaths - not slow and prolonged illness, and certainly not a population of ill, vengeance-seeking victims. Moreover, if terrorists experimented with radioactive contaminants, they could not stop the continuing effects of their actions. It has not been the way of terrorists to kill hundreds and thousands of innocent people."[16]

J. Bowyer Bell too supported the view of Jenkins. Bell wrote in 1978, that "(T)here is no evidence, that the terrorists want to kill a large number of people; but, what they want is media exposure and the exposure of killing a large number of people by using WMD. Moreover, the technological capacities of these terrorist organisations are not adequate to launch attacks by using such weapons. The mix of motive, military and technological skills, resources, and perceived vulnerability does not exist."[17]

In recent years, however, these long-standing assumptions have increasingly been called into question by terrorist attacks that have either crossed the threshold into the domain of WMD use.[18] Since the Japanese cult Aum Shinrikyo led by Shoko Asahara had released sarin gas on Tokyo subway in 1995, nations have been very much worried by the probability that terrorist might use weapons of mass destruction against them. For example, just one month after the September 11 incident, near about eighty per cent of Americans, as per ABC News poll, were worried about terrorist use of chemical or biological weapons in the United States[19]. In October 2001, approximately sixty-three per cent of respondents told pollsters that they apprehend that the use of chemical or biological weapons was the most significant threat from terrorist right now, nine per cent said that they thought the most significant threat right now was from nuclear bomb or dirty bombs, and only just 5 per cent were of the view that the most significant threat came from planes be hijacked and crashed.[20]

As earlier said that the term weapons of mass destruction indicated broadly three types of weapons namely chemical, biological and nuclear weapons. All these types of weapons are significantly different from each other in terms of lethality, in the ease of their deployment and their usefulness to terrorists.

The Chemical Weapon

The use of the chemical weapon is not new; the notion of using toxic gases against the opponent state first occurred in the 1870s to the Fenians. They planned to spray poisonous gas in the House of Commons in London. Likewise, during the Boer War and the Japanese War with Russians in 1905, the plan to use chemical weapons were constructed though not exceeded beyond the experimental stage. The use of gas for the first time on a massive scale was executed in the year 1915 by the Germans in the war of Ypres. Chlorine gas was used in this war, and consequently, approximately five thousands people were killed and many injured.[21]

Meanwhile, the use of phosgene and mixtures of phosgene and chlorine was introduced into the war. The mustard gas was also used.

Though the psychological impact was huge, yet poison gas has no conclusive consequence in any significant battle, irrespective of the fact that hundreds and thousands of soldiers as well as civilians were killed. By the end of the WW I, nearly twenty-five poison gases was used.[22]

The perception that chemical weapons might be employed in future at the time of war came into the minds of the great men of that period as a result thereof in the year 1907, at Hague a peace conference was held, and the signatories of the protocols contracted not to use warheads dispersing asphyxiating and poisonous gases. The use of the toxic gases was also banned by the Geneva Protocols of 1925, which were signed mainly by the European powers.

However, the weak point of these protocols was that it had no specified provisions mentioning what sanctions and steps could be taken if any of the signatories violates the very provisions of these protocols. There was apprehension in the right-thinking people of the global that these protocols were not sufficient to control or banned the use of chemical warfare, and their apprehension turned into reality. During the 1930s, Ethiopia severely suffered because of chemical weapon used by Itlay. Thereafter, almost, all the powers after that equipped themselves to tackle such inhumane attack.[23]

In the initial stage of WW II, the chemical weapons were not used. Hitler, who was himself a sufferer of such weapon during WW I was not in favour of using such a weapon. However, Hitler used chemical weapons when the tide of war turned against him. By the year 1944, the Germans had a massive arsenal of nervous gas bombs. In the end, poison gases were employed by the Germans authorities only against the civilians, in the extermination camps of Eastern Europe - especially against Jewish civilians. Since WW II, poison gas has been used mainly in the Middle East, particularly in Iraq and Iran.[24]

As far as the use of chemical weapons by terrorists are concerned, they can have access to it as these weapons are cheap and easy to obtain; Experts say that the technical knowledge and experience needed in manufacturing chemical weapon is much less than nuclear weapons or biological weapon and even a graduate student can manufacture it. However, the most unmanageable business is sprinkling the weapon orderly. These weapons can also be, to a great extent, hazardous to operate and tough to regulate. Therefore, terrorist do not favour this weapon, although over the years, many terrorist groups have access to chemical weapons and some of them have used it also.

There are several incidents where terrorists had used chemical weapons in order to achieve their end. The glaring example is of Aum Shinrikyo group using sarin gas in the Tokyo subway. The Aum Supreme Truth group is an apocalyptic doomsday cult founded by Asahara Shoko which was responsible for the sarin gas poisoning of the Tokyo subway system on 20 March 1995. The organisation had extensive, comprehensive, elaborate and modern technical facilities. Masami Tsuchiya, Aum's eminent scientist, who confessed to having created the sarin, commented that he had joined the organisation because the organisation has well-equipped laboratory facilities.[25]

Before 20 March 1995 sarin gas attack on the Tokyo subway system, the Aum group had practised for five years and made nine attempts to deploy botulinum poison via airborne dispensers against target though no casualty occurred. Two further failed attempts followed the March attack. After testing the homemade sarin against the Japanese city of Matsumoto on 27 June 1994, killing seven civilians and injuring one hundred fifty people, the sect then deployed it in the Tokyo subway system. In the Tokyo subway attack, twelve people died, and over 5,000 were injured. Following the March attack, Asahara was arrested on 16 May 1995, and it was found that this group was progressing itself to attain the biological weapons as well as nuclear weapons to be used against their opponents.[26] Likewise, in the year 1990, the Liberation Tigers of Tamil Eelam (LTTE) released containers of liquid chlorine to gas Sri Lankan army forces. While this attack succeeded in killing and immobilising, many soldiers shifting winds caused several LTTE units to suffer from the same chlorine gas.[27]

There are many reports which state that al-Qaeda before September 11 attack was interested in acquiring the chemical weapons, and it is on such basis of reports United States on August 20, 1998, charged al-Qaeda with chemical weapons at the al-Shifa pharmaceutical factory in Khartoum, Sudan. The United States bombed the factory, killing one worker and injuring at least twelve others. However, later it was found that the information received by the United States by such reports was not accurate, and the attack was based on inaccurate reporting. The factory owner, Salah Idris, filed suit against the U.S. government claiming damages. In response the U.S. Treasury released Idris's American bank accounts, thereby acknowledging that the administration lacked the evidence to justify their action against him.[28]

There were various other reports too in the 1990s revealing that at-Qaeda is designing and developing chemical weapons, particularly cyanide. The reports stated that makeshift laboratories were in existence in Khost, Jalalabad and Charassiab, district of Afghanistan. More often it was reported that Osama bin Laden had bought and acquired the chemical and biological weapons from the former Soviet states. Some reports stated that bin Laden had bought more than three Chemical and Biological Weapon factory in the former Yugoslavia and had hired several Ukrainian biologists and chemists to train his members. Ahmad Rassam, who pleaded guilty to plotting bomb at Los Angeles International Airport, claimed in court that he witnessed a dog being gassed with cyanide. These claims confirmed with an al-Qaeda video broadcast on CNN showing dogs being killed by toxic chemicals, probably a crude nerve agent or hydrogen cyanide gas.[29] By arresting nine Moroccans in February 2000, the Italian government stated that they had foiled the plan of these terrorists to poison the water supply of the United States embassy in Rome using a cyanide compound.[30] However, when U.S. forces invaded Afghanistan, they only found evidence of very primitive laboratory facilities.

An al-Qaeda computer that fell into the hands of Wall Street Journal reporter Alan Cullison in Kabul contained information of a project, code-named 'Curdled Milk', that was under the direction of that was under the supervision of Ayman al-Zawahiri and included plans to launch a chemical and biological weapons programme. With the arrest of Khalid Sheikh Mohammad in 2003, enough information about the development of this programme was acquired. As per reports, seized documents give evidence that al-Qaeda had the requisite material to develop cyanide and two biological toxins and was close to producing anthrax bacteria. Other reports which came after the September 11 also revealed that al-Qaeda members were being trained in secret camps near Baghdad in how to use Chemical and Biological weapons by experts from a secret Iraqi military intelligent unit.[31]

Though undoubtedly terrorists display a keen interest in acquiring and using chemical weapons, and there is not much evidence which shows that they will attain it easily and use it frequently. The experience shows that not only manufacturing these chemical weapons requires scientific knowledge, well-equipped laboratory, expert scientists but also the expertise and preciseness in executing them, it is, therefore, though not impossible but difficult for terrorists to use them and give preference to chemical weapons over their successful traditional weapons.

Biological Weapons

As far as the history of biological weapons is concerned, it is much older than chemical weapons, but the biological agents that snarl us today are of the new-age invention. The horrific plague of the fourteenth century, which is said to have killed near about one-third of the European population, was allegedly set abroached by the Tartars beleaguering the fortress of Caffa in the Crimea. The Tartars propelled plague-infected (contaminated) bodiess into the citadel; as per the available information, vessels from Genoa conveyed the infection to northern Italy and the other parts of Europe. Another frequently cited illustration of early biological warfare occurred during the Indian wars in North America in the year 1760. It was reported that local British commanders in Pennsylvania schemed to distribute the Indians blankets infected with smallpox vires as a gift; as a result, thereof people faced severe difficiulities due to smallpox epidemic.[32]

During WW I, It was alleged that Germans tried to spray cholera bacilli in Italy, the plague in St. Petersburg, and anthrax in Mesopotamia and Rumania. Though the use of these biological weapons does not produce the desired results, it was termed as unsuccessful, but research and stock pilling continued after the World War I. Almost all the powerful nations indulged themselves in manufacturing the biological weapons, but only the Japanese carried out biological warfare, dropping plague-infested fleas and grains over Chinese cities after the invasion of 1937. However, during the last phase of WW II, the creation of biological weapons was accelerated.[33]

After the Second World War, the nations, sturdy as well as weaker, secretly involved in manufacturing the biological warfare. Iraq, under Saddam Hussein, was particularly active in manufacturing such weapons. Iraq, however, was not the sole country in the Middle East to produce biological weapons. The countries such as Iran, Syria, and above all, Libya was reported to involve in manufacturing biological weapons along with Iraq. It is just not the middle east countries that were engaged in manufacturing these weapons, but as per United States Department, "yellow rain," an agent difficult to classify but belonging to the general family of the mycotoxins, was employed in Laos, Kampuchea, and Afghanistan by Communist forces. There is much evidence to show that KGB was not hesitant in using the biological agents. In the 1970s, the sophisticated agent called ricin were employed two Bulgarian émigrés, Georgi Markov in London and Vladimir Kostov in Paris.[34]

Though no significant incidents of the use of biological weapons by the terrorists have been reported so far, yet there are some instances which reveal that terrorists have access to these weapons. On 24 April 1997, the delivery of a foul-smelling envelope with the word "anthrax"(Sic) scrawled on it not only led Washington D.C., fire department to shut down the B' nai B' rith headquarters but also caused two B' nai B' rith employees to experience what they thought were the symptoms of anthrax infection.[35] Exactly a week after September 11, five letters containing anthrax were mailed to media outlets in the United States. Three weeks later two further letters were mailed, this time to two Democratic senators.[36] Altogether by mid-November 1997, five persons died from inhalation anthrax, and seventeen cases of anthrax exposure were confirmed after over 5000 people had been tested for anthrax infection.[37]

Al-Qaeda's continued interest in biological weapons and particularly in ricin is proved by several arrests in Europe associated with the discovery of traces of the toxin and instruments for its manufacture. These include the arrest of Menad Benchallai in December 2002, known as 'the chemist', he developed ricin and stored it in Nivea face cream jars before giving them to a chemist for safekeeping. Authorities believe that there are interconnected cells of

North Africans attempting to develop ricin operating in France, Britain and Spain.[38]

The fact that biological weapon has many advantages over the other weapons as they are easy to obtain, undetectable, cheap and likely to cause more damage than other weapons, moreover, they tend to suffer humans as well as damage the economy of a country for instance by damaging the crops. With all these advantages, biological weapons are not used much by terrorist groups because of the reason that these biological weapons are sensitive to high and low temperature and affected by the change in wind direction. Moreover, they have a limited life span, and the mode of contaminating foodstuff and other things requires technical knowledge in order to gain the desired result. Thus, it is unlikely to be used by the terrorist organisation, though not impossible; indeed, they can use to blackmail the government in order to make their demand fulfilled.

Nuclear Weapon

The Nuclear weapon, the most lethal weapon in the present era, also comes under the category of the weapon of mass destruction. After the explosion of atom bombs over Hiroshima and Nagasaki, the world at large become speechless and breathless by experiencing the severe damage and pain suffered by the people of Japan. After the WW II, the people of the United States and Western Europe were dominated by the fear of nuclear bomb explosion, and they had the fear that they will be the next target of these lethal nuclear bombs; on the other side, the people of Eastern Europe and those belonging to the third world were least bothered about it. However, in the present scenario, almost every right-thinking person is worried about the safety of his body, property and his country. This worry is not baseless but stands on firm footing as in the present era, and the terrorist groups are more versatile than before, they do not hesitate in using any weapon to fulfil their aim or goal.

During the period of the cold war, there was a cut-throat competition between the two superpowers the United States and the Soviet Union to acquire the nuclear weapons, and there was always the possibility of using these weapons against the other in order to dominate the world. However, with the disintregration of the Soviet Union, the possibility of using nuclear weapons against the other diminished. In the meantime, many other nations too acquired nuclear weapons and the technique of manufacturing nuclear weapons. Thus, the probability that states who sponsor terrorism may use nuclear weapon has increased much more in the present era as compared to the era of the cold war.

The phenomenon of nuclear terrorism is "neither a single entity nor a narrow category."[39] It skirts a wide range from low-level incidents of hazards which involve radioactive substance through raids on the reactors to a detonation of a fully furnished terrorist nuclear bomb.[40] By and large, the terrorist may use nuclear weapon by various means and methods. They can use it by stealing and exploding the nuclear weapon, and they can attack and destroy the nuclear facility, power plant research laboratory or medical facility where radioactive substances are used and by the manufacturing of 'dirty bombs' by illegally acquiring the radioactive substances.[41]

To gain an assembled nuclear weapon, terrorist organisations may aim at any of the hundreds and thousands of nuclear weapons germinated in the national stocks of the United States, Russia, France, England, India, Pakistan and China. Terrorist groups can easily avail the opportunity of acquiring the nuclear weapons as the number of states possessing the nuclear weapon is increasing and the new members of the nuclear club are apt to waive or violate the standard norms of safeguards.

As per the Report of the International Task Force on Prevention of Nuclear Terrorism, a particular problem area lies in the widespread deployment of tactical nuclear weapons: "There have been published reports of one terrorist group in Europe has tried unsuccessfully to obtain information on NATO nuclear-weapon storage facilities, and of another having sought unsuccessfully to enlist the help of a nuclear scientist regarding nuclear weapons, they considered stealing. One national leader, regarded as being engaged in sponsoring terrorism, is reported to have sought unsuccessfully to buy nuclear weapons while pursuing a nuclear research programme that could be applied in the long term to making bombs."[42]

The risk of 'loose nukes' had been a constant concern to the world at large since the end of the Cold War. The worry was that the disintegration of the Soviet Union would facilitate trafficking in nuclear weapons. There was considerable worry about the ability of safety in Russian nuclear facilities. There are also worries about the niggardly paid Russian scientists might strive to sell their knowledge or some of the contents of their laboratory.

Moreover, the amount of nuclear material present in other nations is expanding, and what is more worrying is that most of the countries not have a proper security system. Many countries having nuclear weapon use Permissive Action Link (PAL) system designed to ensure maximum safety and security of their weapons.[43] The nuclear weapon of the countries such as the United States, Britain, France and Russia are safeguarded using all these Mechanisms. However, several countries having nuclear capabilities do not have robust security mechanism.[44] Though the chances of smuggling or theft of nuclear weapons from these countries are very less, however, probabilities of causalities cannot be denied. Another point to be noted is the capability of the terrorist organisation to manufacture a nuclear weapon. To fabricate its nuclear weapons, a terrorist organisation requires expertise, and such expertise and skill is widely available to them. In the year 1977, the Office of Technology Assessment (OTA) produced a report entitled, "Nuclear Proliferation and Safeguards." After a general account of the two basic methods of assembling fissile material in a nuclear explosive, the report stated that "Militarily useful weapons with useful weapons with reliable nuclear yields in the kiloton range can be constructed with reactor-grade plutonium, using low technology." Moreover, "given the weapons material and a fraction of a million dollars, a small group of people, none of whom had ever had access to the classified literature, could possibly design and build a crude nuclear explosive device."[45]

Approximately three years before the OTA report, a book by Mason Willrich and Theodore Taylor revealed astonishing facts. He stated that "The design and manufacture of a crude nuclear explosive is no longer a difficult task technically, and a plutonium dispersal device which can cause widespread radioactive contamination is much simpler to make than an explosive." On March 22, 1978, in a statement presented to the Senate Committee on Governmental Affairs, Dr Taylor elaborated on his views: "Given the required amounts of special nuclear materials, in a variety of chemicals and physical forms, it is highly credible that a group of people could design and build fission explosives, using information and non-nuclear substances that are available to them. In a few situations, it is quite possible that this could be done by one person working alone. Such explosives could be transported by automobile. Their probable explosive consequnces would depend upon the knowledge and skills of the person or group."[46]

For many years, Taylor's views worrying about the terrorist manufacturing of nuclear explosives was challenged. However, on March 15, 1978, he showed a draft manuscript on the design and manufacture of nuclear weapons, written by Dimitri Rotow, an undergraduate student. This manuscript, entitled "Nuclear Weapon Design and Construction", was written without any expert assistance and access to specific national security information or restricted or secured data. Reviewing the efforts of a twenty-two-year-old student, Dr Taylor, commented: "Mr Rotow's manuscript is the most extensive and detailed exposition than I have seen outside the classified literature. Although it contains several errors, these do not generally detract from his main lines of reasoning in setting down a variety of approaches to the design of a variety of types of fission weapons. I was surprised by the volume of well-organized information and the number and the class of designs he was capable of collecting in a time that he says was about three months of intensive work. I would say his exposition is much stronger in dealing with design principles, and the reasoning behind them, than or estimates of performance, in which I found significant errors. All in all, however, I was neither shocked nor surprised than an intelligent and innovative person without extensive training in nuclear physics could produce such a document, though I was surprised that it took so little time. His work certainly tends to confirm a conviction I have held for more than twelve years."[47]

One such terrorist group attempt to build nuclear weapon was the Japanese terrorist group Aum Shinrikyo which tapped its vast financial resources to buy Australian properties and conducted on investigation for purchasing uranium- enrichment technologies.[48] However, it failed because enrichment is an extremely challenging process, requiring state-level resources. The apprehension has been strengthened with the revelation of the A.Q. Khan network. Apart from this, it is said that al Qaeda too had the access and ability to use a nuclear weapon. Before September 11, there were several reports that Osama bin Laden had acquired nuclear weapons. In the case that the United States brought against bin Laden for the embassy bombings, prosecution witness Jamal Ahmad al-Fadl testified that as early as 1993-94 he had been charged by al-Qaeda with acquiring uranium in Khartoum. In August 1998, a leaked Israeli intelligence report stated that bin Laden had paid over two million sterling for a "suitcase' bomb to a middleman in Kazakhstan. A few months later Russian intelligence service informed their American counterparts that bin Laden had given a group of Chechens thirty million in cash and two tons of opium in exchange for twenty nuclear warheads.[49] In September 1998, a member of al-Qaeda group, Mamduh Mahmud Salim, was arrested in Germany for trying to obtain highly enriched uranium for al-Qaeda.[50] There were other reports of expensive failed efforts by bin Laden to acquire enriched uranium in Eastern Europe. In December 2000 Arab Security sources alleged that a shipment of about twenty nuclear warheads originating in Kazakhstan, Turkmenistan, Russia and Ukraine had been intercepted in route to bin Laden.[51]

Reports after September 11 are more astonishing and threatening. A report in November 2001 claimed that al-Qaeda had acquired a Russian-made suitcase nuclear bomb from central Asian sources. The device is reported to weight eight kilograms and to possess two kilograms of fissionable uranium and plutonium. The report said the device, serial number 9999, was manufactured in October 1998 and could be set off by a mobile phone. On February 8, 2004, the Egyptian newspaper Al-Hayat reported that al-Qaeda had bought tactical nuclear weapons from Ukraine in 1998 and was holding them in storage; the Ukrainian government denies the claim and insists that they transferred all nuclear weapons Russia by 1996. On several occasions, bin Laden and al-Zawahiri have claimed to have nuclear weapons. In an interview in early 1999 with Time Magazine bin Laden asserted that acquiring any weapon, including chemical, biological and nuclear ones, is a 'religious duty.' This assertion has been invoked at a regular interval of times to demonstrate his determination to obtain these weapons. He said: "Acquiring weapons for the defence is a religious duty of Muslims. If I have indeed acquired these weapons, then I thank God for enabling me to do so. Moreover, if I seek to acquire these weapons, I am carrying out a duty. It would be a sin for Muslims not to try to possess the weapons that would prevent the infidels from inflicting harm on Muslims.'[52]

Further bin Laden made his posture more clearly on weapons of mass destruction: "We do not consider it a crime if we tried to have nuclear, chemical, biological weapons ... We have the right to defend ourselves.'[53]

Moreover, a Pakistani reporter, Hamid Mir, claims to have interviewed bin Laden in November 2001 and to have heard him assert: "We have chemical and nuclear weapons as a deterrent, and if America used them against us we reserve the right to use them.' In March 2004 Ayman al-Zawahiri went much further. He told Hamid Mir that al-Qaeda possessed nuclear weapons purchased in central Asia. He stated that "if you have $30 million then there is no problem going into the central Asian black market, getting in contact with some penniless Soviet Scientists and purchasing lots of compact nuclear weapons."[54]

There is, however, absolutely no evidence, to conclude that al-Qaeda has nuclear weapons, but their interest in possessing such weapons was found. A London Times reporter discovered a blueprint for a 'Nagasaki bomb' in files in an abandoned al-Qaeda house in Kabul. The 'Super bomb' manual, as it was called, discusses the advanced physics of nuclear weapons and dirty bombs. Thus, it can be asserted that al Qaeda had thought or desired to have to nuclear bomb.[55]

Certain evidences suggest that they possess the technology to manufacture nuclear weapons. However, it is a challenging job for the terrorists to utilise such weapons as it involves technical complexities and vast resource which they cannot afford.[56] Hence an attack with a full-fledged nuclear weapon may seem unlikely in the near future. Nevertheless, the acts of nuclear sabotage, by radical ecologists' albeit on a minor scale, took place during the 1970s and 80s. In 1973 a commando associated with the leftwing Argentinean group, the ERP, intruded at the project site of the Atucha atomic power station situated at Buenos Aires.

In 1976, an attack was lunched at the nuclear power plant situated at Britany in France. Subsequently, Lemoniz nuclear power station in

Bilbao, Spain, was attacked by the ETA, the Basque separatist organisation. Few more assaults were made against nuclear plants near San Sebastian, Pamplona, Tafalla, Beriz, and other sites in northern Spain. The attackers murdered the head of the Lemoniz plant and abducted the chief engineer.

In the year 1979, a nuclear instrument industrial unit in Spain was attacked. In 1982, the terrorist wing of the African National Congress (ANC) damaged two South African nuclear plants, causing considerable damage. Both nuclear reactors were damaged, however as they were not operational at that particular time, hence there was no emission of radiation.[57] Though directly using a nuclear weapon is next to the impossible task, but nuclear sites can be sabotaged and damaged easily, as evidenced by these incidents mentioned above.

International Law & Weapon of Mass Destruction

Though the probability of using weapons of mass destruction is much smaller, however, the use of WMD has never been ruled out. The United States National Strategy for Combating Terrorism (2003), alarmed that, ".... probability of terrorist organisation using chemical, biological, radiological, or nuclear weapon....has increased significantly during the past decade."[58] While celebrating Indian Independence Day, the defence minister of India, Pranab Mukherjee and National Security Advisor, M.K. Narayan raised the worries over the intelligence news that Lashkar-e-Toiba (LET) is eyeing to attack the nation's nuclear installations.[59]

Moreover, the WMD in the hands of rogue states and nuclear experts like A.Q. Khan furthers the worry of international society and the fact that even if the terrorists have not the expertise to manufacture and detonate the weapons of mass destruction, possibility is there that they can sabotage the laboratory, nuclear plants where the work is going on or where these weapons are stored under the strict suppression of state and create considerable loss to a nation, not in terms of economy but also in terms of life and environment.

However, the world is not a passive onlooker. The rise in the importance of weapons of mass destruction on security and foreign policy framework in the last few decades compelled to examine the plan and action of international law in this field.

The international law since the late nineteenth century has been making efforts to control the use of weapons of mass destruction. Though there is no specific treaty or convention which deals with the problem of terrorists using and manufacturing the weapons of mass destruction, much effort has been made in controlling the use and manufacturing of weapons of mass destruction by the states.

The Declaration of St. Petersburg of 1868 constitutes the most kernel principle of the laws of war, which stated that the states do not have the absolute right to injure and harm the belligerent. The Declaration notably prohibits the use of weapons, which cause unnecessary and excessive suffering. The Declaration of St. Petersburg stands both for the principle that military necessity cannot override the laws of war, and for the notion that warfare, is governed by laws of humanity that are valid even without the concern of governments. This Declaration manifestly prohibits the states from using such weapons which can cause immense disaster and unknown sorrow for humans as well as other creatures of the Earth.[60] The Declaration of July 29, 1899 (hereinafter First Hague Declaration of 1899) reaffirmed the principle contained in the declaration of St. Petersburg. In Article 22 of the Regulations annexed to the Fourth Hague Convention of 1907 confirms the basic principle of the laws of war that the right of belligerents to adopt means of injuring the enemy is not unlimited. Article 23 (a) of this Declaration stated that it is especially forbidden to employ poison or poisoned weapons. However, the terms poison or poisoned weapons were not defined. Furthermore, Article 23 (e) of the Hague Regulations of 1907 prohibits the use of arms, projectiles or material calculated to cause unnecessary suffering. Since the weapon of mass destruction are calculated to cause unnecessary suffering but also the devastation of the highest and unimaginable magnitude which the world has never witnessed before the use of such weapon is prohibited.[61]

The Geneva Gas Protocol of 1925 not only prohibits the use of asphyxiating poisonous or other gases but also of all analogues liquids, materials and devices. This Protocol is so comprehensive in its prohibition that it includes any weapon whose effects are similar to that of poisonous gas or bacteriological warfare. This Protocol was concluded on June 17, 1925, under the auspices of the League of Nations, after reciting the desire to make the prohibition of the poisonous gas as a past of International Law. The Protocol is binding only upon the contracting parties and that too within the limits of reciprocity. Those states which are not parties to the Protocol may consider themselves bound by the Convention voluntarily. However, again in an army conflict between Iran and Iraq which began in September 1980, chemical weapons were used by both the parties, even though both the states were parties to the Geneva Protocol of 1925.[62]

Both The Hague Declaration and Geneva Protocol are, however, insufficient and weak arm control agreement. Firstly, these instruments neither regulated the state competence to manufacture and accumulate chemical and biological weapons as the agreements were confined only to restrictions on the use of such weapons and secondly, the constraint on the use of both agreements was not absolute and compulsive. The Hague Declaration prohibits the use of chemical weapons applied only in the case of war between contracting parties. The prohibition was not binding if a non-contracting party joined the conflict as a belligerent. Likewise, the Geneva Protocol's prohibition applied only in armed conflict between state parties. Moreover, many state parties made reservations declaring that the ban would not bind them in the situation where another state party violates the prohibition during armed conflict. The Geneva Protocol reckoned in effect, a prohibition on the first use of chemical and biological weapons.[63]

The other important Convention which talks about the prohibition of WMD is The Convention on the Prohibition of the Development, Production and Stockpiling of Bacteriological (Biological) and Toxic Weapons and on Their Destruction, which was adopted in 1972. The Convention on the Prohibition of Military or Any Other Hostile Use of Environmental Modification Techniques (ENMOD Convention) of 1977. The Convention on Prohibitions or Restrictions on the Use of Certain Conventional Weapons which May be deemed to be Exclusively Injurious or to Have Indiscriminate Effects (Inhumane Weapons Convention) 1980. The Convention or the Prohibition of the Development, Production, Stockpiling and Use of Chemical Weapons and on their Destruction 1993. The Convention on the Prohibition of the Use, Stockpiling, Production and Transfer of Anti- Personnel Mines and on their Destruction 1997. The Convention on the Physical

Protection of Nuclear Material (Nuclear Material Convention), 1979. International Convention for the Suppression of Terrorist Bombing 1997.

The international legal developments are not adequate to tackle the growing WMD threat. Antiterrorism treaties and conventions did not specifically begin to incorporate WMD terrorism until the 1990s, which reflects the growth of worry about the probability of catastrophic terrorism. There are only two conventions which concern about WMD terrorism. The UN Convention on the Suppression of Terrorist Bombings, and the proposed Draft UN Convention for the Suppression of Acts of Nuclear Terrorism. The UN Convention on the Suppression of Terrorist Bombings follows the standard law enforcement approaches which are mentioned in other antiterrorism treaties: state parties criminalise certain offences, take jurisdiction over the commission of such acts, agree to prosecute or extradite alleged perpetrators, and participate in law enforcement cooperation and assistance. The principal object of this convention is to increase the potential that terrorist acts will be punished and thus deter terrorist activity.[64]

The other developments on the issue of WMD and terrorism are the Security Council Resolution 1373 of September 28, 2001, which stated that all the UN members are obliged to fight against terrorism, and this resolution contains numerous obligations on UN member states relating to combating terrorism. The Resolution 1373 was followed by the Security Council Resolution 1540 of April 2004. This Resolution is a cornerstone in the international efforts to control WMD terrorism. The UN Security Council Resolution 1540 affirmed that the proliferation of WMD to terrorists threatens international peace and security. As Resolution 1540 was adopted under Chapter VII of the UN Charter and enjoyed widespread support, and can play an essential role in encouraging partner capacity building to combat WMD terrorism. The Resolution mandates that ".... all states shall refrain from providing any form of support to non-state actors that attempt to develop, acquire, manufacture, possess, transport, transfer, or use nuclear, chemical, or biological weapons and their means of delivery." Resolution 1540 reminds us that the proliferation of the world's most dangerous weapons to the world's most dangerous actors requires states to take on new duties if they wish to remain in good standing within the international community.[65]

Though a great effort has/had been made to control and reduce the threat of WMD terrorism, after going through various international legal accomplishments, a critical approach reveals cleavage that continues to exist in our legal framework against WMD terrorism. For example, there is an urgent need to secure not only adoption but also satisfaction, moreover complete national implementation of the Nuclear Terrorism Convention and the Amendment to the Convention on Physical Protection of Nuclear Materials. We should not remain content with the criminalisation of acts of WMD terrorism, which is the main object of both the Nuclear Terrorism Convention and the International Convention for the Suppression of Terrorist Bombing. The comprehensive legal studies in most of the conventions in many ways a 'Pre atomic' document, and their provisions were fashioned before states recognised the possibility of instant and overwhelming use of WMD by the terrorist groups. Though there has yet been no clear legal standard framed to prevent the terrorist attacks or the use of WMD, it is the duty of the states to discourage the use of WMD. Further, the threat of WMD terrorism can be prevented and controlled in this global world, when all the nations with practical, integrated, and sustainable capabilities, come together at one platform without any ulterior motive to protect and promote the welfare of the humankind.

Notes

1. Walter Laquer, "Weapon of Mass Destruction", Pamala L. Griset, and Sue Mahan (ed.), *Terrorism in Perspective*, (2003), p. 239.
2. *Ibid.*
3. Gus Martin, *Understanding Terrorism: Challenges Perspective and issues*, (2006), p. 353.
4. *Ibid.*
5. *Ibid,* p. 354.
6. *Ibid,* p. 355.
7. Bruce Hoffman, *Terrorism and Weapons of Mass Destruction : An Analysis of Trends and Motivations*, (The RAND Corporation,p.8039-1), p. 9.
8. *Ibid.*
9. *Ibid.*
10. Brian Michael Jenkins, *International Terrorism: The Other World War*, (The RAND Corporation, R-3302-AF), (1985), p. 12.

11. *Ibid.*
12. Bruce Hoffman, *Terrorism and Weapons of Mass Destruction: An Analysis of Trends and Motivations*, (The RAND Corporation P-8039-1), (1999), p. 12.
13. Robert L. Beckman, "Rapporteur's Summary", Alexander and Loventhal (eds.), *Nuclear Terrorism: Defining the Threat*, (1986), p. 13.
14. Brian M. Jenkins, "Is Nuclear Terrorism Plausible?" Alexander and Leventhal (eds.), *Nuclear Terrorism: Defining The Threat*, (1986), p. 13.
15. *Ibid.* p. 15.
16. Brian M. Jenkins, *Will Terrorists Go Nuclear?* (1975), p. 6-7.
17. Bowyer Bell, *A Time of Terror: How Democratic Societies Respond to Revolutionary Violence,* (1978), p. 121.
18. Bruce Hoffman, *Terrorism and Weapons of Mass Destruction: An analysis of Trends and Motivations*, (RAND Corporation, P-8039-1), (1999), p. 16.
19. ABC News Poll, October 8-9, 2001, PolloingReport.com, Terrorism (8), at http://www.pollingreport.com/terror8.htm. Accessed on Feburary 14, 2006.
20. Fox News/Opinion Dynamics Poll, September 8-9,2002, PollingReport.com, Terrorism (5), at http://www.pollingreport.com/terror5.htm. Accessed on February 14 2006.
21. Walter Laquer, "Weapons of Mass Destruction" Pamala L. Griset, Sue Mahan (eds.) *Terrorism in Perspective*, (2003), p. 242.
22. *Ibid.*
23. *Ibid.,* p. 243.
24. *Ibid.*
25. See, Sean K. Anderson and Stephen Sloan, *Historical Dictionary of Terrorism*, (2002), p. 72, and, Lousie Richardson, *What Terrorists Want: Understanding the Terrorist Threat*, (2006), p. 191.
26. *Ibid.*
27. *Ibid.,* p. 504.
28. BBC News.com, 'Factory Bombing: A Matter of Evidence' 5 may, 1999.
29. Louise Richardson, *What Terrorists Want: Understanding the Terrorist Threat*, (2006), p.192.
30. Eric Croddy, 'Chemical Terrorist Plot in Rome?', *CNS Research Story*, March 11, 2002.
31. Louise Richardson, *What Terrorists Want: Understanding the Terrorist Threat*, (2006), p. 193.
32. Walter Laquer, "Weapon of Mass Destruction", Pamala L. Griset, and Sue Mahan (ed.) *Terrorism in Perspective*, (2003) p. 245.
33. *Ibid.*
34. *Ibid.* p. 246.
35. Sean K. Anderson and Stephen Sloan, *Historical Dictionary of Terrorism*, (2002), p. 49.
36. Louise Richardson, *What Terrorists Want: Understanding the Terrorist Threat*, (2006), p. 194.

37. Sean K. Anderson and Stephen Sloan, *Historical Dictionary of Terrorism*, (2002), p. 49.
38. Joby Warrick, 'An Al- Qaeda "Chemist" and the Quest for Ricin', *Washington Post*, May 5, 2004.
39. Sita Kanta Mishra, "Nuclear Terrorism: Myth and Reality", Chintamani Mahapatra and Amulya Tripathy (ed.) *Transnational Terrorism: Perspective on Motives and Measures and Impacts*, (2007), p. 357.
40. Gavin Cameron, *Nuclear Terrorism: A Threat Assessment for the 21st Century*, (1991), p. 1.
41. Sita Kanta Mishra, "Nuclear Terrorism: Myth and Reality", Chintamani Mahapatra and Amulya Tripathy (ed.) *Transnational Terrorism: Perspective on Motives and Measures and Impacts*, (2007), p. 358.
42. H.B. Mishra, *Terrorism: Threat to Peace and Harmony*, (1999), p. 164-165.
43. Sita Kanta Mishra, "Nuclear Terrorism: Myth and Reality", Chintamani Mahapatra and Amulya Tripathy (ed.), *Transnational Terrorism: Perspective on Motives and Measures and Impacts*, (2007), p. 364.
44. Ferguson, "Nuclear smuggling: How Serious a Threat?", Strategic Forum banner, Number 59, January 1996, at http://www.ndu.edu/inss/strforum/SE_59/forum59.html. Accessed on 26 January 2005.
45. H.B. Mishra, *Terrorism: Threat to Peace and Harmony*, (1991), p. 170.
46. *Ibid.,* p. 170-71.
47. *Ibid.,* p. 171.
48. See, "The Demand of Black Market Fissile Material"' at http://www.nti.org/e-research/cnwm/threat/demand.asp.
49. Louise Richardson, *What Terrorists Want: Understanding the Terrorist Threat*, (2006), p. 200.
50. Benjamin Weiser, 'US says bin Laden Aide Tried to Get Nuclear Weapon', *New York Times*, September 26.
51. Louise Richardson, *What Terrorists Want: Understanding the Terrorist Threat*, (2006), p. 200.
52. *Ibid.,* p. 203.
53. Peter L. Bergen, *Holy War: Inside the Secret World of Osama bin Laden*, (2001), p. 92.
54. Louise Richardson, *What Terrorists Want: Understanding the Terrorist Threat*, (2006), p. 203.
55. *Ibid.,* p. 201.
56. Sita Kant Mishra, "Nuclear Terrorism: Myth and Reality", Chintamani Mahapatra and Amulya Tripathy (eds.) *Transnational Terrorism: Perspectives on Motives, Measures and Impacts*, (2007), p. 366.
57. Walter Laquer, "Weapons of Mass Destruction" Pamala L. Griset, Sue Mahan (eds.) *Terrorism in Perspective*, (2003), p. 252.
58. See, The US National Strategy for Combating Terrorism, February 2003, p. 9, at http://www.whitehouse_gov/news/releases/2003/02/counter_terrorism/counter_terrorism_strategypdf. Accessed on 26th April 2006.

59. "India's nuke installations on LeT hit list: Mukerjee", at http://www.nwes.monstersandcritics.com/india/article_1185448.php/Indias_nuke_installations_on_LeT_hit_list_Mukerjee. accessed on July 31, 2006.
60. Gurdeep Singh, *International Law*, (2003), p. 466. and H.O. Agarwal, *International Law and Human rights*, (2006), p.556.
61. Gurdeep Singh, *International Law*, (2003), p. 466. and H.O. Agarwal, *International Law and Human rights*, (2006), p.556.
62. H.O. Agarwal, *International Law and Human Rights*, (2006), p.557.
63. David P. Fidler, "International Law and Weapons of Mass Destruction: End of the Arms Control Approach?" at www.law.duke.edu/shell/cite.pl?14+Duke+J.+Comp.+&+Int'l+L.+39+pdf. Accessed on 12 November 2006.
64. *Ibid.*
65. Multipronged Approach Needed to Keep Weapons from Terrorists, available at http://www.useu.usmission.gov/Article.asp?ID=39FE81A3-1243-4EE7-9099-1EB19AD62497.

Chapter - 6

Global Terrorism and International Legal Regime

Introduction

According to Kofi Annan, "Terrorism is a global threat with global effect; its consequences affect every aspect of the United Nations agenda – from development to peace to human rights and the rule of law. By its very nature, terrorism is an assault on the fundamental principles of law, order and human rights, and the peaceful settlement of disputes upon which the United Nations is established. The United Nations has an indispensable role to play in providing the legal and organizational framework with which the international campaign against terrorism can unfold."[1]

The whole world is burning because of the inhumane nature of terrorism. Terrorism is the cause for killing hundreds of innocents in different incidents ranging from blowing Indian plane 'Kanishka', Lockerbie disaster to September 11 attack on World Trade Centre, 2008 Mumbai attack, Boston Marathon Bomb Blast in 2013, Paris attack on 13th November 2015, Bangladesh attack in 2016 and more recently Sri Lanka attack in 2019. However the concept of global terrorism or International terrorism reached at its zenith after the September 11, 2001 attack on the United States of America and all nations facing this problem came together to combat terrorism under the leadership of United States of America.

Our world has become more unified and interconnected. Commerce and technology have brought people more close to each other, and the world is termed as a global village. Mc Donald's sells hamburgers in India and Indian music and videos can be heard and seen in remote corners of the world. Problems and their solutions are no longer isolated geographically[2]. Terrorism too with time became international. International terrorism is terrorism that spills over on to the world's stage. Targets are selected because of their value as symbols of international interests, and the impact that attacks against these targets will have on a global audience. International terrorism is a form of psychological warfare intended to create a reaction on the parts of its audience, and protracted warfare being carried out for political aims, with or without the sponsorship of the state[3]. International terrorism occurs when the target is an international symbol, and when the political, psychological effects go beyond a purely domestic agenda. International terrorism has two essential qualities; one it is a methodology that is selected explicitly by violent extremists, and second, it is an identifiable brand of terrorism.[4] Terrorists now have a wide range of ever more effective weapons at their disposal and have developed modern techniques of persuasion.

The crime of terrorism unveils the number of difficulties of a legal nature. One of the significant problems lies in the definition of terrorism. Some thinkers are of the view that the crime of terrorism is not a domestic problem, and the international community should interfere. While some argue that labelling terrorism as crime and adopting counter-measures may have unwanted consequences resulting in human rights violations. Furthermore, it is complicated to answer whether terrorism can solely be dealt with by criminal law, and it is justifiable to use armed force against terrorists.[5]

The fight against terrorism is now multifaceted and includes standards applied by the UN Security Council, including financial sanctions.[6] However, the foremost model to counter-terrorism remains criminal law, and the acts of terrorism, in one or the other form, constitute criminal offences. The difficulty with the application of criminal law faced at international and domestic level is to classify and define who is a terrorist and who is not. In the present scenario, terrorists can be prosecuted in an international criminal court if their acts amount to war crimes or crimes against humanity. It is high time that terrorism should be included within the jurisdiction of the International Criminal Court. Terrorism is not a legal concept that can be analysed in such a manner that it is possible to define it in a straight jacket fashion.

Development of International Co-operation Against Terrorism

The League of Nations, its successors United Nations along with some international and regional organisation, realised the gravity of the problem took steps towards the eradication of the problem in one way or the other.

In the 20th Century, the assassination of several politicians, during the interwar period led negotiations within the League of Nations. The League of Nation unanimously adopted a resolution in December 1934, appointing a committee of Experts curb down the growing menace of terrorism around the world. In November 1937, two conventions were adopted, The Convention for the Prevention and Punishment of Terrorism and The Convention for the Creation of International Criminal Court. The former convention defined acts of terrorism as 'criminal acts directed against a State and intended or calculated to create a state of terror in the minds of particular persons, or a group of persons or the general public' and listed acts to be criminalised by States Parties, including those causing death, severe injury or loss of liberty to heads of State and public officials, damage to public property of another State, and risk to the lives of members of the public. However, the most surprising fact was that though the world community, on the one hand, recognised terrorism as a growing global problem, on the other hand, they never recognised these conventions, the first convention received only one ratification, that of India in January 1941[7]. Since then terrorism has been addressed issue by issue, in response to particular outrages.

United Nations and Terrorism

Terrorism which once considered being the problem of one or two nations very soon regarded as a global problem. Though much attention had not been paid at an initial stage, and the United Nations in the first two decades of the last century has also been painfully slow and adopted piecemeal approach in dealing with the menace of terrorism. The attack on the World Trade Centre changed the entire international strategic equation and the movement for the eradication and combating of terrorism through the medium of international law gathered momentum. The United Nation, with time, adopted resolutions and declarations to tackle the problem of terrorism. Comprehensive measures to combat individual terrorism have, to some extent, been the victim of the deflection of international attention towards State terrorism and the use of force.

The failure of the League of Nations to avert a second world war did not destroy the conviction, shared by many, that only by some form of the general organisation of states could a system of collective security be achieved which would protect the international community from the scourge of war[8]. Moreover, as a result of this definite conviction on October 24, 1945, the United Nations was ultimately established.

After the establishment of the United Nations, no specific convention on the terrorism as such has been adopted, nor does the U.N. Charter contain any specific provision on it. It was in the year 1972 when terrorist attacked at the Olympic Games at Munich, the General Assembly of the United Nations put terrorism on its agenda on the initiative of the then Secretary-General Kurt Waldheim. The agenda was entitled as: "Measures to prevent terrorism and other forms of violence which endanger or take innocent lives or jeopardise fundamental freedoms and the studying of the underlying causes of those forms of violence which endanger to take innocent lives or jeopardise fundamental freedoms and the study of the underlying causes of those forms of terrorism and act of violence which lie in misery, frustration, grievance and despair and which cause some people to sacrifice human lives, including their own, in an attempt to effect radical changes".[9]

The long title of the agenda (resolution) indicates the cautious attitude of the international community, which not only dealt with the methods to curb down terrorism but also with the causes of terrorism[10]. Although the committee constituted by the General Assembly to define terrorism met until 1979, yet it did not reach any agreement. There was dissent as to whether acts committed by national liberation movements for causes such as decolonisation should be excluded from any definition of terrorism, and arguments were also made not to impose an international ban on terrorist activities unless the causes of the terrorism were acknowledged and resolved.

The unfeasibility of achieving international consensus on the universal definition of terrorism led to a piece-meal approach to cooperation to prevent and criminalise terrorist acts. International agreements were negotiated on specific areas of terrorist activity. From the 1960s onwards, the international community has adopted the United Nations General Assembly has adopted thirteen global conventions related to the prevention and suppression of international terrorism, as well as several resolutions on terrorism.[11]

These International conventions set out obligations on states: to define acts of terrorism as criminal offence; to prosecute individuals suspected of such offence; investigate such offences and extradite suspects upon request and provide mutual legal assistance on request. Apart from these conventions, Vienna Declaration and Programme of Action 1993 also condemned the acts, methods and practices of terrorism in all its forms and manifestations which are aimed at the destruction of human rights, democracy and threatening the security and integrity of states.[12]

The UN sixth (legal) committee and Ad-hoc Committee established under the 1996 UNGA Resolution 52/210[13], are currently continuing their work to that end by negotiating the Comprehensive draft Convention on International Terrorism[14]. This convention has yet not come into existence as on 11 August 2016. These conventions have a common objective to prosecute and prevent acts of terrorism by imposing obligations on State parties to assist in criminal and extradition proceedings. In their provisions on extradition, the three recent agreements, unlike old ones, specify that the offence in question may not be regarded as a political offence for extradition or mutual legal assistance.[15] As most of the terrorist acts are politically motivated, this removes the loophole by which terrorists could escape extradition and confirms that terrorism cannot be justified, whatever the objective is.[16]

The United Nations Security Council is also active and playing a pivotal role in eliminating the evil of terrorism, and it has defined international terrorism as a threat to international peace and security. Security Council adopted Resolution 731 (1992), criticising and implementing sanctions against Libya; when Libya was deaf to the request of extradition of suspected bombers of an aeroplane[17], and in resolution 1070 (1996) which was adopted against Sudan the Security Council reaffirmed that 'the suppression of acts of international terrorism, including those in which states are involved, is essential for the maintenance of international peace and security.'[18]

It was, however, the 11 September 2001, the attack upon the World Trade Centre that moved this process on a higher level. In resolution 1368 (2001), which was adopted the following day to combat by all means threats to international peace and security caused by terrorist attack', unequivocally condemned the attack and declared that it regarded such attacks 'like any act of international terrorism, as a threat to international peace and security'. Resolution 1373 (2001) reaffirmed this proposition and the need to combat threats to international peace and security caused by terrorist acts by all means as per the charter,[19].

The Security Council while acting under Chapter VII of the UN Charter made several binding decisions demanding states to work for the prevention and suppression of the financing of the terrorist act, freezing of the financial assets and economic resources of persons and entities involved in terrorism. States were also called upon to abstain itself from providing any assistance and support to those persons who are involved in terrorist activities and take harsh action against them, and the state should cooperate with other states in preventing and suppressing terrorist acts. Further, the Council declared that acts, methods and practices of terrorism were contrary to the purposes and principles of the United Nations and knowingly planning, financing and inciting terrorist acts were also contrary to the purposes and principles of United Nations. More importantly, the Council established a Counter-Terrorism Committee (CTC) to monitor implementation of the resolution. States were asked to report to the committee on steps and measures they had taken to implement the resolution[20]. However, the weakest point of the Resolution is that it contains no definition of terrorism. Resolution 1373(2001) has been criticised as the Security Council has gone beyond its previously determined Charter powers and has trespassed jurisdiction exercised by the General Assembly and agreement negotiated there. Despite that, the resolution has been accepted in practice, albeit reluctantly, and is a crucial part of the international counter-terrorism effort.

The Security Council made another resolution 1377 (2001) while affirming the earlier proposition, it declared that acts of international terrorism constitute one of the most severe threats, to international peace and security in the twenty-first century', and requested the counter-terrorism committee to assist in the promotion of best practice in covered by resolution 1373; including the preparation of model laws, to examine the availability of various technical, financial, legislative, and other programmes to facilitate the implementation of resolution 1373[21].

Apart from these resolutions, an Ad-hoc Committee was set up by the United Nation's General Assembly, and in the year 1994, a Declaration on Measures to Eliminate International Terrorism was adopted through General Assembly resolution 49/60. This declaration condemned all acts, methods and practices of terrorism, as criminal and unjustifiable, wherever and by whomever. Committed, nothing that ' criminal acts intended or calculated to provoke a state of terror in the general public, a group or person or persons or particular persons for political purposes are in any circumstance unjustifiable, whatever the considerations of a political, philosophical, ideological, racial, ethnic, religious or any other nature that may be invoked to justify them'. States are obliged to refrain from organising, instigating, facilitating, financing or tolerating terrorist activities, and to take practical measures to ensure that their territories are not used for terrorist installations, training camps or the preparations of terrorist acts against other states. States are further obliged to apprehend and prosecute or extradite perpetrators of terrorist act and to co-operate with other states in exchanging information and combating terrorism[22].

In the year 1996, a supplementary declaration was adopted, which emphasised besides that acts of terrorism and assisting them are contrary to the purposes and principles of the United Nations Charter. The United Nation's General Assembly has also adopted several resolutions (e.g. resolution 34/145, 35/168 and 36/133) calling for ratification of the various conventions and improvement in cooperation between states in this area[23].

United Nation Office on Drugs and Crime (UNODC) is yet another office connected with the United Nations, which is playing a vital part in preventing and combating the menace of terrorism. To strengthen the efforts of United Nations in preventing and suppressing the evil of terrorism, UNDOC has an expanded programme of work for technical assistance to counter-terrorism which is based on the principles suggested by the United Nations Commission on Crime Prevention and Criminal Justice and approved by General Assembly. The mandates, carried out by UNDOC's Terrorism Prevention Branch (TPB) with the Division for Treaty Affairs (DTA), include the provision of technical assistance and advisory services to countries in their fight against terrorism. This is done by providing legislative assistance to countries, which makes them become the parties to, and implement the Universal anti-terrorism Conventions and Security Council Resolutions (1373)[24].

There are several organisations, including the United Nations working for the protection of human beings, but they are helpless in combating this evil. The newly established International Criminal Court (ICC) is the next step in this process, which is formed to punish acts against humanity. The success of ICC is very dim in combating the crime of terrorism as it has no jurisdiction on this subject-matter.

International Criminal Court and Terrorism

Broadly terrorism can be classified: (1) Terrorism from Above and (2) Terrorism from Below. Terrorism from Above means terrorism practised by the state directly or sponsored by state indirectly, by quasi-governmental agencies and personnel against perceived enemies. States sponsors terrorism at two levels, one at the domestic level and the other at the international level. The "Terrorism from Below" is committed by non-state movements; groups against governments, ethnonational groups, religious groups and other perceived enemies.[25] The indulgence of states and non-states actors in sponsoring terrorism is one of the greatest concerns. However, the Rome Convention focuses only on four categories of core crime and ignored crimes of terrorism which have a huge influence on people throughout the world and global economic development.[26] Like core crimes, the crime of terrorism has the actual or potential trans-boundary effect or maybe intra-State and offend a fundamental value of the international community,[27] but it is excluded from the Rome Statute. Van der Vyver, remarks that terrorism was deliberately omitted from the subject matter jurisdiction of the ICC, partly because the United States approached the very first session of the Ad Hoc Committee on a permanent International Criminal Court with the express object of excluding the crime of terrorism from the proposed subject matter jurisdiction.[28] The key reason for the United States to request this specific omission was its deep concern that the inclusion of the crime in this international tribunal could undermine its extensive investigative efforts undertaken in its national prosecutions of international terrorists.[29] Nevertheless, during the Rome Conference many States like Spain, Algeria, Sri Lanka, India, Barbados etc., submitted proposals to indeed include terrorism in the jurisdiction provision of the ICC[30], but ultimately, because these supporters for the inclusion of terrorism could not be able to convince large enough number of delegates to support the proposal and also because there was no consensus definition among the States and required elements of the crime, terrorism was excluded from the Rome Statute. The crime of terrorism may in the future be dealt under international crimes within the jurisdiction of an international court[31] if States are of the view that the values they conflict with are sufficiently significant to the international community and that international prosecution is an effective way of dealing with them.[32] The records from the Rome Conference reveal six reasons underlying the rejection of the suggested terrorism provision.[33] The first hindrance was the lack of a clear and universally accepted definition of terrorism.[34] The second reason was the notion that the three core crimes represented the crime of greatest concern to the international community, and terrorism does not raise this level of international concern.[35] The third ground for rejecting the inclusion of terrorism under the jurisdiction of ICC was a desire not to overburden the ICC and the need for gravity threshold.[36] The fourth reason against the inclusion of terrorism in the Rome Statute was that such an inclusion would create obstacles in the acceptance of the Rome Statute.[37] The fifth argument was that some States questioned the need to include terrorism in the Rome Statute as there was already in place a system of international cooperation to deal with it in the form of treaty crime.[38] Moreover, the sixth and last objection to the inclusion was that since terrorism is such a politically-sensitive term, and if ICC would deal with cases of terrorism it will be forced into the political realm, and its legitimacy and credibility will be in question.[39] All reasons but one against the inclusion of terrorism within the jurisdiction of ICC seem not credible. How the international community as a whole and states individually addressing the terrorism can lead to the conclusion that presently terrorism is as severe as other international crime described in the Rome Statute.[40] Moreover, comparing the status of the Genocide Convention to that of the Terrorism Financing Convention reveals that while the former has forty-one signatories and 141 parties; the latter has 132 signatories and 173 parties. Adding to this, the Security Council has affirmed that acts of terrorism constitute threats to international peace and security.[41] The claim that ICC will be overload if terrorism will be included is baseless as in Rome Statute there is a built-in mechanism[42] which will ensure that the ICC will have the jurisdiction over the most cruel terrorist acts just like it has jurisdiction over the most severe crimes against the humanity or any other crimes.[43] The concern that inclusion of terrorism will impede the acceptance of Rome Statute is irrelevant at present as an amendment to the Rome Statute does not apply automatically to all the states parties but rather applies to only those states that have ratified it specifically.[44] The reason that a system of international cooperation exists to deal with terrorist acts is not a stretch of thought a good reason to exclude from the jurisdiction of ICC. For example, genocide, a core crime, was also under the regime of an international treaty which was already in existence. Moreover, most of the war crimes under the Rome Statute were already dealt with the Geneva Conventions.[45] Inclusion of terrorism will force ICC into the political realm should not preclude ICC to exercise its jurisdiction over terrorist acts as even with other crimes; the ICC is not sheltered from concerns of politicisation. In 2010, the Member States included crime of aggression within the jurisdiction of ICC, a matter that was not resolved in the Rome Conference. In the present scenario where the non-state actors are operating from the sovereign territory of certain failed states; where most of the armed conflicts are non-international; and low-intensity armed conflicts in the Middle East involves the crime of aggression with the interference of international politics-a case of violation of state's sovereignty.[46] Moreover, all international crimes involve political sensitiveness to a certain extent and this argument can be raised with any of the respective core crime. Only one issue is a real impediment that is lack of an acceptable definition of terrorism. A review conference in 2010 defined aggression but did not pursue a 2009 Dutch proposal on terrorism.[47] As of 2016, terrorism is yet to be included in the ICC's jurisdiction.

Definition of Terrorism

The crime of terrorism is the indefinable concept.[48] The difficulty in defining terrorism is not new. Bassiouni has persistently stated that the fundamental problem is a failure at the international level to reach a working definition of terrorism.[49] None of the twelve global agreements defines terrorism except the Terrorist Financing Convention, and that is only for a secondary purpose.[50] The impediments of arriving at unanimity on a definition for the cause of a global prohibition of terrorist acts pertain to two related questions: are there causes which justify acts otherwise categorised as terrorism, which should, therefore, be excluded; and should 'State terrorism' be included?[51]

Cooper, remarks that "there has never been since the topic began to command serious attention, some golden age in which terrorism was easy to define." Writing about terrorism in the middle of the 1970s, the political historian Walter Laquer threw up his hand; he viewed that providing a comprehensive definition was virtually impossible because of the great variety of circumstances in which this type of violence had appeared and the numerous and often competing political causes whose advocates had used it. Martha Crenshaw, another leading observer, wrote that the absence of a consensual definition continued to plague those interested in studying terrorism[52]. The hurdles of having a consensus definition raise the question of whether the effort is worthwhile. It will be more significant not to waste energy and time in defining terrorism and let the world community focus to revert to the range of acts that all States regard as impermissible in all circumstances.[53] However, the definition of terrorism is needed if there is to be a complete international prohibition on terrorism and a prerequisite for multilateral cooperation, including extradition. A definition is also required if terrorism is to be added to the domain of the International Criminal Court. Moreover, prevailing instruments enforcing obligations about counter-terrorism need a definition to ensure uniform enforcement and effective monitoring.[54] Nevertheless, what follows is a war of words, fought in a mass media, as each side denies that its behaviour constitutes terrorism as struggles to reach the moral high ground. More often, the mass media compound the confusion by applying the term 'terrorist' on a highly selective basis. Newspapers back and forth usually refer particular group as extremists, militants, guerrillas, 'terrorists' depending upon exceptionally hazy criteria[55]. As a consequence thereof, the pervasive and indiscriminate use of often politically convenient label of 'terrorism' continues to mislead this field of inquiry.[56]

The phrase 'one man's terrorist is the other man's freedom fighter' poses a serious problem in defining terrorism. The boundary between legitimate dissidence and freedom-fighting or terrorists and terrorist activity is a difficult one which involves a question of perspective and which is vulnerable to changes in judgment over history. Despite the vast publicity and long history of the phenomenon of terrorism, there is no single comprehensive definition of the term terrorism. More than a hundred definitions of terrorism exist, but none of them is universally accepted. Some definitions specifically include religious motivations; others include hate, millenarian and apocalyptic groups. Several definitions refer only to non- state actors, whereas others include state-sponsored terrorism. Terrorism by groups is an essential part of several definitions, but some definitions include terrorism by individual actors[57]. Diversity is inherent to the international legal system and division between States on a particular issue is unavoidable. However, as terrorism is predominantly an international phenomenon, consensus is essential to counter this menace.[58]

In 1996, India initiated a Draft International Convention on the Suppression of Terrorism (Draft Comprehensive Convention)[59] which created some hope to form an agreed definition and unite the international counter-terrorism mechanism under one instrument. However, the Draft Comprehensive Convention is still under debate. Article 2 of the Terrorist Financing Convention sets forth the prohibition on the various forms of financing terrorism. The definition is twofold. Article 2(1)(a) refers to acts previously prohibited in prior international conventions related to terrorism, and Article 2(1)(b) refers to any other act of terrorism[60]. Article 2(1)(b) does not deal with the identity of the perpetrator and thus may be applied to both state as well as no-state actors. This definition is wide and broad and is suitable to address cyber-terrorism and future manifestations of terrorism.[61] Many of the Convention even do not mention the word terrorism, thus illustrating the view that the offence of terrorism can be curbed down without specifying terrorism as an offence.[62]

While drafting a definition of terrorism, human rights considerations have to be taken care of.[63] As these offences are likely to carry higher penalties than other offences, national systems may have more invasive means of investigation for terrorist offences, the political offence exception may not be applied, and application for asylum may be refused. If the definition of terrorism is comprehensive and includes even less serious nature of criminal acts, there is an apprehension that serious consequence of being a terrorist suspect in national law will be applied to criminals who otherwise are not terrorists.[64] While an internationally accepted definition of terrorism is still awaited, human rights concerns have encouraged the 'UN Special Rapporteur on the promotion and protection of human rights and fundamental freedoms while countering terrorism' to convey that a definition of terrorism be restricted to acts causing death or serious bodily injury or taking the hostages, provided that these acts are within the scope of the global agreements and are committed with the intention of provoking a state of terror, intimidating a population, or compelling a government or international organisation to action or inaction.[65] Though this approach is appealing in eliminating the problem created by international or national definitions that are too wide in scope, it may not be supported by the international community.[66]

After 11 September 2001, there have been more straight-forward criticism of terrorism by the United Nations. UN Security Council Resolution 1373 (2001) declared: "...that acts, methods, and practices of terrorism are contrary to the purposes and principles of the United Nations and that knowingly financing, planning and inciting terrorist acts are also contrary to the purposes and principles of the United Nations."

However, UNSC Resolution 1377 (2001) of 12 November 2001 moderately nuanced the wording signifying that it was international terrorism that conflicted with the purposes and principles of the United Nations, not all terrorism. However, subsequent Resolutions have dealt with acts of terrorism in similar ways that were ostensibly domestic.[67] There is no simple answer to the question of how to balance rights, in the same way, there is no agreed definition of terrorism. In practice, terrorism is still just a blanket term for any violent acts, and there is no agreement, in the first place, as to what constitutes terrorism. Consensus at an international level is still some distance ahead.[68] However, a ray of light occurred when Special Tribunal of Lebanon[69] dared to venture into hitherto judicially avoided legal territory and dived straight into the exact definition of terrorism as discreet crime.[70] However, the definition given by the Special Tribunal of Lebanon was not free from discrepancies as it is both under-and-over inclusive.[71]The new ICC would have had terrorism within its scope, but its terms of reference were redefined and limited, to the exclusion of these offences. Thus no new international criminal remedy will exist in respect of these offences, and the opportunity to redefine and refine was missed due to political impediments.[72]

Terrorism as a Part of Core Crimes Under Jurisdiction of ICC

Another problem is whether terrorism is appropriately or adequately addressed alone by the criminal law or whether it is needed and legitimate to use armed force against terrorists. The attacks in the US on 11 September 2001 were described as ‘armed attack’ within the of Article 51 of the UN Charter.

Consequently, the US and UK used military force in self-defence against Al-Qaeda and the Taliban, violating all minimum standards of international humanitarian law and human rights.[73] Perhaps such a response to terrorism has made the situation more critical and sensitive. The fight against terrorism is now multi-faceted. However, the predominant standard to tackle terrorism remains criminal law, and terrorist acts, in one or other forms, constitute criminal offences. However, the application of criminal law at the national and international level remains one of the significant problems as the international community still debating on a consensus definition of terrorism.

Terrorist acts can be prosecuted in an international court if they amount to war crimes or crimes against humanity. Only one internationalised court, the Lebanon Tribunal has jurisdiction over terrorist acts, but these are crimes under Lebanese, not international law. In order that international court or tribunal which has authority to determine cases related to terrorism, a terrorist act may fall within the categories of crimes against humanity or war crimes. The structured use of terror was acknowledged as both a war crime and a crime against humanity by the Nuremberg Tribunal.[74]

The offences considered by the terrorism Conventions were included in the list of treaty crimes in the ILC draft for the new international court and got some support at the time of negotiations for considering terrorism to be under the jurisdiction of ICC. However, this was not achieved, because the world community was of the view that prevailing treating providing for national prosecutions was adequate, and the international community failed to negotiate agreed definition of terrorism. Resolution F of the ICC Final Act recommended that a review conference examine crimes of terrorism 'to arrive at an acceptable definition and their inclusion in the list of crimes within the jurisdiction of the court'.[75]

Alarming terrorist activities around the globe necessitates the world community to have a definition of terrorism accepted by all without which ambiguities, and as a result, thereof shortcomings are created that allow terrorists to slip through the chinks in the law, particularly in international law with its underlying principle of *nullum crimen sine lege*, where clarity and certainty about prohibited conduct is significant. The current scenario leads to grey areas which can be exploited by terrorists. All States condemns terrorist activity, and international law prohibits such activities and as international law imposes obligations an all states to follow and respect the rules of international law, it can be said that the States cannot adopt insouciant approach in defining the act of terrorism because such an approach makes international institution weak to punish and prevent terrorist act.[76]

Terrorism as War Crime

It is wrong to argue that terrorism can legally only be considered as a criminal offence in time of peace. International humanitarian law prohibits acts of terrorism and may amount to war crimes. Article 51(2) of Additional Protocol I of 1977 provide: "The civilian population as such, as well as individual civilians, shall not be the object of attack, and prohibits acts of threat of violence the primary purpose of which is to spread terror among the civilian population".[77] This prohibition and criminalisation are part of customary international law.[78] The same acts are prohibited in non-international conflict by Article 13(2) of Additional Protocol II. Both provisions are part of wider prohibitions on attacks against civilians. Article 4(2)(d) of Additional Protocol II further prohibits 'acts of terrorism' in non-international conflicts. The acts of terrorism find mention in the list of violations of common Article 3 in the Statutes of the ICTR and the Sierra Leone Special Court,[79] while ICTY had no such expression in the Statute. Nevertheless, the Tribunal has ruled that it has authority because of the general provision of Article 3 of its Statute.[80] Article 8 of the ICC Statute, which describes war crime excludes terrorism and therefore, ICC does have jurisdiction concerning terrorism. In the ICC, attacks on civilians carried on with the specified intent to terrorise will be an element in sentencing only.[81]

In the first-ever case related to terrorism before an international court, the ICTY convicted General Galic on the war crimes charge of 'acts of violence the primary purpose of which is to spread terror among the civilian population', based upon command responsibility for a prolonged military operation of shelling and sniping in civilian areas of Sarajevo.[82] The Tribunal found that the campaign was intended to terrorise the civilian population.[83] The war crime does not consist in causing terror; it is to be expected that all acts of war will result in terror in the concerned country. The spreading of terror does not have to be the only purpose of the acts, but it does have to be the primary purpose.[84] In the *AFRC* case, the SCSL ruled that use of child soldiers, abduction and forced labour were committed primarily for military purposes and thus did not constitute the war crime of terrorism, while the brutal amputations of hand or arms of civilian were committed primarily to spread terror.[85] In totality, the international case law illustrates that there are three elements in the war crime of acts of terrorism: (i) acts or threat of violence; (ii) the accused willfully made the civilian population or individual civilians not taking direct part in hostilities the objects of those acts or threats of violence; and (iii) the acts or threats were carried out with the specific intent of spreading terror among the civilian.[86] The Rome Statute of the ICC does not include any war crimes of terrorism within jurisdiction. Therefore, acts of terrorism or spreading terror amongst the civilian cannot be prosecuted as such. However, as pointed by the ICTY in *Galic*, such acts may be regarded as specific instances of the general prohibition of attacks on civilians, breaches of which are within the ICC's jurisdiction.

Terrorism as a Crime Against Humanity

Terrorist acts are even not listed as crimes against humanity in the Statutes of the ad hoc Tribunals or the ICC. Nevertheless, if the acts fall within the list of constituent crimes and if their executions are extensive or structured (and, in case of the ICC, are 'against any civilian population'), they will fall within the ambit of definition of crimes against humanity in all of the Statutes. They cannot be excluded only for the reason that they are executed to terrorise people and with a particular political or ideological motive. In the ICTY case of *Galic*, the accused was charged with and convicted of crimes against humanity of murder and inhumane acts based on the same facts as the war of crimes.[87] The perception that terrorism could be included as a crime against humanity has received extensive support in legal literature. However, it is a controversial and complicated issue to include terrorism under the category of crime against humanity and much depends on the question of whether the terrorist assault meets the contextual elements of the crime against humanity. Article 7 of the Rome Statute defines a crime against humanity as an act which is part of a widespread or systematic attack, directed against a civilian population, with knowledge of the attack.

Moreover, for the ICC to have jurisdiction, the attack must be 'under or in furtherance of a State or organisational policy'. The phrase 'State or organisational policy' is the most significant hurdle in enlarging the ambit of crime against humanity and including in it the act of terrorism. The non-state actors may also carry out the crime against humanity.[88]

After 11 September 2001, terrorism was condemned as crimes against humanity.[89] Undoubtedly, there were no problems with any submission that the crimes should, therefore, be tried by the ICC as the State primarily concerned was opposed to such an idea and the doctrine of complementarily would have stood in the way even if there was otherwise jurisdiction. However, the acts may well have been within the subject-matter jurisdiction of the ICC.[90] The germane issue is what degree of organisational adroitness those non-state actors should attain in order to come within the ambit of Article 7. The organisational requirements for the evaluation of crimes against humanity are responsible command, control over part of territory and proficiency to trigger an armed conflict.[91] A non-state group which lacks these capabilities would fail to qualify as a perpetrator of crimes against humanity.

Terrorism and Genocide

Terrorism and genocide are two forms of violence, having increasing attention towards the end of the 20th century. Terrorism and genocide can be differentiated in relation to the sources of violence. Terrorism is carried out by the state as well as non-state actors and in recent times, Abu Bakr al-Baghdadi's ISIS would be the classic example of terrorism by non-state actors. In the case of genocide, violence is backed by the state and can be referred to as state terrorism. Glaring example of distinction between terrorism as violence of non-state actors and genocide as the violence of a state is the Israeli-Palestinian conflict which developed initially from the clash of two nationalisms in the 19th century.[92] There is an essential link between these two kinds of violence. Often a state fighting against terrorism proceeded to carry out acts of ethnic cleansing against the section of the population perceived to be producing terrorists. The most impressive example that shows up this link between terrorism and genocide can be found in Kosovo. In Kosovo there was a peaceful, non-violent Gandhian civil disobedience movement led by the Kosovar Albanian leader Ibrahim Rugova during the decade of the 1980s, campaigning for the restoration of Kosovo's special status in Serbia. This was met with an iron-fisted response from the Serbian leader Slobodan Milosevic in the form of repressive police laws designed to end all these activities. The consequent was that subsequently the militant organisation, the Kosovo Liberation Army (KLA) emerged in 1996. The point is that counter-terrorism measures like the one Milosevic and Bush administration used often create more terrorists then they are capable of putting down.[93]

Conclusion

Terrorism is one of the most present-day severe challenges that the world is facing, and the States have tried to response the threat of terrorism by assorting treaties at the national, regional and international level. At the international level, the world is fragmented and suffers from lack of coherence. The diverse perspective of States has created obstructions to arrive upon an adequate definition. Every State acknowledges the fact that terrorism is an international issue and almost all the States around the globe have the definition of terrorism in their domestic laws with little or no difference and regional organisations defines terrorism with slight differences of words here and there but, unfortunately, a definition of terrorism agreed by States is still not in existence acknowledging the fact that the fight against terrorism cannot be succeeded without a globally accepted definition, even then the States are failing to arrive at any consensus definition. Perhaps it is a fundamental problem which has to be looked upon seriously if the world community truly wants to curb this evil. The fight against terrorism cannot be a wild, unjust war. The proper response to the definition of terrorism should be that the definition of terrorism ought to be outside the political realm. The lack of adequate agreed-upon definition justifies States not to fulfil their international obligations.

If International criminal law is to develop and gain respect amongst the international community, then the focus must be on bringing persons on trial, not on extra-judicial killings that can be justified by extending the scope of the international law of armed conflict that was never intended to cover "sporadic acts of violence". The jurisdictional reach of ICC has to be investigated, and jurisdiction of the ICC should be expanded by including terrorism as a separate crime as the law of defence as enshrined in Article 51 of the Charter of the United Nations cannot be invoked against non-state actors in the strict sense.

Gradually there is a depletion of the gap between international core crime and terrorism, which gives space to consider that terrorism could be the fifth category of crime on which ICC can have the jurisdiction. The motivation to include terrorism as a distinct crime under the jurisdiction of the ICC springs from two sources. One, the Special Tribunal for Lebanon has propounded an authoritative definition of terrorism in peacetime under customary international law and two most terrorist attacks cannot be qualified as core crimes under ICC.[94] The preamble of the Rome Convention states that protection of civilians and other vulnerable groups from heinous crime is the main object and purpose of the ICC and the world community by rectifying various conventions related to terrorism has acknowledged that terrorism is a real threat to the humanity. The definition should not impede fighting against the evil of terrorism. It would make no sense to acknowledge the sufferings of civilians while denying the ICC the jurisdiction to take action against the perpetrators of terrorism. The world community should be united to include terrorism under the jurisdiction of ICC and add another tool to fight against terrorism.

Notes

1. Kofi Annan, UN Secretary General, addressed to General Assembly on 4th October 2002.
2. Margaret Atwood, 'International Terrorism, Pamala L. Greiset and Sue Mahan (eds) *Terrorism in Perspective*, (2003), p. 49.
3. Sean K. Anderson and Stephen Sloan, *Historical Dictionary of Terrorism*, (2002), p. 481.
4. Gus Martin, *Understanding Terrorism: Challenges Perspective and Issues*, (2006), p. 272.
5. Christine Gray, *International Law and the Use of Force*, 3rd edn. (2008); Juttee Brunee and Stephen Toope, 'The Use of Force after Iraq' (2004) 53 ICLQ 537; Sean Murphy, 'Terrorism and the Concept of "Armed Attack" in Article 51 of the UN Charter' (2002) 43 *Harvard International Law Journal* 41.
6. See John P. Grant, 'Beyond the Montreal Convention' (2004) 36 *Case Western Reserve Journal of International Law* 453 at 472.
7. S.K.Verma,"Terrorism and International law", B.P.Singh Sehgal (ed.), *Global Terrorism Socio-Politico and Legal Dimensions*, (2002), p.343; Ben Saul, 'The Legal Response of the League of Nations to Terrorism' (2006) 4 *JICJ* 78; , Cryer, Friman…[et.al.], *An Introduction to International Criminal law and Procedure*, (2010).
8. D.W. Bowett, *The Law of International Institution*, (1977), p. 21.
9. Hans Koecher, "The United Nations, The International Rule of Law and terrorism", 14th Centennial Lecture, S.C of the Philippines and Philippine Judicial Academy, at [www.i-p-o.org/koechler-un-law-terrorism.pdf]. Accessed on September 12, 2006.
10. *Ibid.*

11. Convention on Offenses and Certain other Acts Committed on Board Aircraft, 1963 (Popularly known as Tokyo convention); Convention for the Suppression of the Unlawful Seizure of Aircraft, 1970; Convention for the Suppression of Unlawful Acts Against the safety of Civil Aviation, 1971 (Popularly known as Montreal Convention, 1971); Convention on the Prevention and Punishment of Crimes against Internationally Protected Persons, 1973; Convention on the Physical Protection of Nuclear Material (Nuclear Materials Convention), 1979; International Convention Against the taking of Hostages, 1979; Protocol for the Suppression of Unlawful Acts of Violence at Airports serving International Civil Aviation, (Supplements the 1971 Montreal Convention), 1988; Convention for the Suppression of Unlawful Acts against the Safety of Maritime Navigation, 1988; Protocol for the Suppression of Unlawful Acts against the Safety of Fixed Platforms Located on the Continental Shelf (Supplement the Rome Convention), 1988; Convention on the Marketing of Plastic Explosives for the Purpose of Detection, 1991; International Convention for the Suppression of Terrorist Bombing, 1997; International Convention for the Suppression of Terrorist Financing, 1999; International Convention for the Suppression of Acts of Nuclear Terrorism, 2005.
12. See Tal Becker, *Terrorism and the State* (2006) at 84-118.
13. The Proposal was made by India in 1996, UNDoc.A/C.6/51/6.
14. "Draft Comprehensive Convention on International Terrorism", at cns.miis.edu/pubs/inven/pdfs/intlterr.pdf. Accesed on 12 September 2006.
15. Art. 11, Terrorist Bombing Convention; Art.14, Terrorist Financing Convention; and Art. 15, Nuclear Terrorism Convention.
16. See, Cryer, Friman…[et.al.], *An Introduction to International Criminal law and Procedure*, (2010).
17. *Ibid*; See Michael Plachta, 'The Lockerbie Case: The Role of the Security Council in Enforcing the Principle Aut Dedere Aut Judicare' (2001) 12 *EJIL* 125.
18. "The Fight against Terrorism: Terrorism and Human Rights" at www.una-uk.org/archive/terrorism/terrorismhr.html. Accessed on 23 sept. 2004.
19. See Mathew Happold, 'Security Council Resolution 1373 and the Constitution of the United Nations' (2003) 16 *LJIL* 593; Paul Szasz, 'The Security Council Starts Legislating' (2002) 96 *AJIL* 901; Stefan Talmon, 'The Security Council as World Legislature' (2005) 99 *AJIL* 175.
20. Malcom N. Shaw, *International Law*, (2005), p. 1051
21. *Ibid.*
22. *Id.*
23. *Id.*, p. 1052.
24. "Implementing international action against terrorism" at www.unodc.org/terrorism.html. Accessed on September 20 2004.
25. Gus Martin, *Understanding Terrorism: Challenges Perspective and Issues*, (2006), p. 111-112.
26. In Res. 56/120 the UN General Assembly expressed deep concern over 'the impact of transnational organized crime on the political, social and economic stability and development of socities'. UN Doc. A/RES/56/120(2002); See,

Cryer, Friman...[et.al.], *An Introduction to International Criminal law and Procedure*, (2010).

27. See Neil Boister, 'Transnational Criminal Law?' (2003) 14 *EJIL* 953.
28. Johan D van der Vyver, 'Prosecuting Terrorism in International Tribunals' (2010) *24 Emory International Law Review* 533-535. See also, Harmen van der Wilt, Inez Braber, "The Case for Inclusion of terrorism in the Jurisdiction of the Criminal Court", *ACIL* Research Paper 2014-13, available at www.acil.uva.nl.
29. See United States Comments to Ad Hoc Committee Report, U.N. GAOR, 50th Sess., pp. 27-29, U.N. Doc.A/AC.244/1/Add.2 (1995).
30. Draft Statute of the ICC, Article 5 defines "crimes of terrorism" means: (1) Undertaking, organizing, sponsoring, ordering, facilitating, financing, encouraging or tolerating acts of violence against another State directed at persons or property and of such a nature as to create terror, fear or insecurity in the minds of public figures, groups or persons, the general public or populations, for whatever considerations and purposes of a political, philosophical, ideological, racial, ethnic, religious or such other nature that may be invoked to justify them; (2) An offence under the following Conventions: (a) Convention for the Suppression of Unlawful Acts against the Safety of Civil Aviation; (b) Convention for the Suppression of Unlawful Seizure of Aircraft; (c) Convention of the prevention and Punishment of Crimes against Internationally Protected Persons, including Diplomatic Agents; (d) International Convention against the Taking of Hostages; (e) Convention for the Suppression of Unlawful Acts against the Safety of Maritime Navigation; (f) Protocol for the Suppression of Unlawful Acts against the Safety of Fixed Platforms located on the Continental Shelf. (3) An offence involving use of firearms, weapons, explosives and dangerous substances when used as a means to perpetrate indiscriminate violence involving death or serious bodily injury to persons or group of persons or popularions or serious damage to property.
31. as in past it had been tried by Lebanon Tribunal.
32. See, Mahmoud Hmoud, 'Negotiating the Draft Comprehensive Convention on International terrorism' (2006) 4 *Journal of International Criminal Justice*, 1013.
33. Eric Bales, Torturing the Rome Statute: the Attempt to Brng Guantanamo's Detainees within the Jurisdiction of the International Criminal Court, *16 TULSA J. COMP & INT'L L. 173, 188* (2009); Lucy Martinez, Prosecuting terrorists at the International Criminal Court: Possibilities and Problems, *RUGHTERS L.J. 1, 18* (2002); Pouyan Afshar Mazandaran, An International Legal Response to an International Problem: Prosecuting International Terrorists, *6 INT'L CRIM. L. Rev.* 503, 528 (2008).
34. Michael Lawless, Terrorism: An International Crime, *HARD. HUM. RTS.* J. 139, 159 (2007-2008).
35. Mark D. Koelsgard, *A* Human Rights Approach to Counter-Terrorism, *36 CAL. W. INT'L L.J.* 249, 286 (2006).
36. Christian Much, The International Criminal Court and Terrorism as an International Crime, *14 MICH. ST. J. INT'L L.* 121, 126 (2006).
37. Aviv Cohen, Prosecuting Terrorists at the International Criminal Court: Reevaluating an Unused Legal Tool to Combat Terrorism, *Michigan State International Law Review, Vol. 20:2*

38. *Ibid*; See Official Records of the Rome Conference, U.N. Diplomatic Conference of Plenipotentiaries on the Establishment of International Criminal Court, 3d plen. Mtg. at 172, p. 25, U.N. Doc. A/CONF.183/13.
39. Luz E. Nagle, Terrorism and Universal Jurisdiction: Opening a Pandora's Box? *GA. ST. U. L. REV.* 339, 361 (2011).
40. Lucy Martinez, Prosecuting terrorists at the International Criminal Court: Possibilities and Problems, *RUGHTERS L.J. 1*, 18 (2002)
41. S.C. Res. 1373, U.N. Doc. S/RES/1373.
42. Article 1 of the Rome Convention states that the ICC will exercise jurisdiction only for the most serious crimes of international concerns; Article 5 of the Rome Statue specifies crimes within the jurisdiction of the ICC.
43. Roberta Arnold, The ICC as a New Instrument for Repressing Terrorism 56 (2004); See Cryer, Friman…[et.al.], *An Introduction to International Criminal law and Procedure*, (2010).
44. *Supra Note* 36.
45. *Ibid.*
46. See, Keith A. Petty, Sixty Years in the Making: The Definition of Aggression for the International Criminal Court, *31 Hasting International and Comparative Law Review.* 531, 532 (2008)
47. ICC Assembly of States Parties, Report of the Bureau on the Review Conference, Addendum, 10 November 2009, Doc. ICC-ASP/8/43/Add. 1, Annex IV, 12-13.
48. See, R.R. Baxter, 'A Sceptical Look at the Concept of Terrorism' (1973/4) 7 *Akron Law Review* 380; R.Higgins and M.Flory (eds.), *Terrorism and International Law* (London, 1997) 28.
49. See Bassiouni, 'A Policy-Oriented Inquiry into the Different Forms and Manifestations of International Terrorism', at pp.xvi in Bassiouni, *Legal Responses to International Terrorism: U.S. Procedural Aspects* (1988); See also Geoff Gilbert, *Responding to International Crime*, (2006).
50. Art. 2 of the Convention refers to the offence of financing acts of terrorism, which are defined as acts covered by the terrorism Convention and 'any other act intended to cause death or serious bodily injury to a civilian, or to any other person not taking an active part in hostilities in a situation of armed conflict, when the purpose of such act, by its nature or context, is to intimidate a population, or to compel a Government or an international organization to do or to abstain from doing any act'.
51. Cryer, Friman…[et.al.], *An Introduction to International Criminal law and Procedure*, (2010); Green, International Crimes and the Legal Process, *29 INT'L & COMP.LQ 567* at p. 582.
52. Leonard Weingberg, *Global Terrorism, A Beginner's Guide*, (2006), p. 1.
53. G. Levit, 'Is "Terrorism" worth defining?' (1986) 13 *Ohio Northern University law Review* 97; John Murphy, 'Defining International Terrorism: a Way out of the Quagmire' (1989) 19 *Israel Yearbook on Human Rights* 13.
54. Cryer, Friman…[et.al.], *An Introduction to International Criminal law and Procedure*, (2010).
55. Leonard Weingberg, *Global Terrorism, A Beginner's Guide*, (2006), p.2.

56. See Bassiouni, 'A Policy-Oriented Inquiry into the Different Forms and Manifestations of International Terrorism', at pp.xvi in Bassiouni, *Legal Responses to International Terrorism: U.S. Procedural Aspects* (1988); See also Geoff Gilbert, *Responding to International Crime*, (2006).
57. Pamala L. Griset, Sue Mahan (ed.), *Terrorism in Perspective*, (2003), p.xii.
58. See Alexandra V Orlova James W Moore, '"Umbrella's" or "Building Blocks"?: Defining International Terrorism and Transnational Organized Crime in International Law' (2005) *27 Houston Journal of International Law* 287-290. See Fiona de Londras, 'Terrorism as an International Crime' in William A Schabas & Nadia Bernaz (eds.) *Routledge handbook on International Criminal Law* (2010).
59. Letter dated Nov. 1, 1996 from the permanent representative of India to the United Nations of the Secretary-General, U.N. Doc. A/C.6/51/6 (Nov. 11, 1996).
60. Article 2(1)(b) of the Convention states – Any other act intended to cause death or serious bodily injury to a civilian, or to any other person not taking an active part in the hostilities in a situation of armed conflict, when the purpose of such act, by its nature or context, is to intimidate a population, or to compel a government or an international organization to do or to abstain from doing any act.
61. *Supra note* 36 Also see Aviv Cohen, 'Cyber Terrorism: Are we Legally Ready? *J. INT'L & L.* 1 (2010).
62. Cryer, Friman…[et.al.], *An Introduction to International Criminal law and Procedure*, (2010).
63. UNGA Res. 48/122 (1993). See also, Terrorism and Human Rights, Second progress report prepared by Ms. Kalliopi K. Koufa, Special Rapporteur, E/CN.4/Sub.2/2002/35, 17 July 2002; Specific Human Rights Issues: New Priorities, in Particular Terrorism and Counter-Terrorism: A Preliminary framework draft of principles and guidelines concerning human rights and terrorism, Expanded working paper by Kalliopi K. Koufa, E/CN.4/Sub.2/2005/39, 22 June 2005; and see Hoffman, *Human Rights and Terrorism*, 26 HRQ 932 (2004).
64. See Vijay P Singh and Subir k Bhatnagar, 'Anti-Terror Laws in India: A Study in Internal Security Mechanism' in Mithilesh N Bhatt (ed) *Terrorism: Its Legal Framework and Beyond*, (2017) 23-45.
65. Report of December 2005 (E/CN.4/2006/98). See also Cryer, Friman…[et.al.], *An Introduction to International Criminal law and Procedure*, (2010); Rodley, 'Can armed opposition groups violate human rights?' in Mahoney and Mahoney, *Human Rights in the 21st Century: A Global Challenge*, (1993), at pp. 297 et seq.
66. See Ben Saul, *Defining Terrorism in International Law* (2006).
67. See, Sossai, The Internal Conflict in Colombia and the Fight against Terrorism: UN Security Council Resolution 1456 (2003) and Further Developments, *3JICJ 253 (2005).*
68. See, Geoff Gilbert, *Responding to International Crime*, (2006); See also Cassese, The International Community's 'Legal' Response to Terrorism, *38 INT'L & COMP.LQ 589* at pp. 605-06 (1989).

69. Established to prosecute bombings in Lebanon in 2005.
70. Manuel J Ventura, 'Terrorism According to the Special Tribunal for Lebanon's Interlocutory Decision on the Applicable Law: A Defining Moment or A Moment of Defining?' (2011) 9 *Journal of International Criminal Justice* 1022.
71. See, Mathew Gillett and Matthias Schuster, 'Fast-track Justice: The Special Tribunal of Lebanon Defines Terrorism (2011), 9 *Journal of International Criminal Justice*, 1005-1014. Also See B. Saul, 'Legislating from A Radical Hague: The UN Special Tribunal for Lebanon Invents an International Crime of Transnational Terrorism', (2011) 24 *LJIL* 677.
72. Claire de Than and Edwin Shorts, *International Criminal law and Human Rights*, (2003) p. 237
73. Christine Gray, *International Law and the Use of Force*, 3rd edn (2008); Juttee Brunee and Stephen Toope, 'The Use of Force after Iraq' (2004) 53 *ICLQ* 785; Sean Murphy, 'Terrorism and the Concept of Armed Attack in Article 51 of the UN Charter' (2002) 43 *Harvard International Law Journal* 41.
74. 'Nurmenberg IMT: Judgement and Sentence' reprinted in (1947) 41 *AJIL* 172 at e.g. 229, 231, 289, 319.
75. The first review conference will be held at least seven years after the entry of the ICC Statute.
76. Michael Lawless, 'Terrorism: An International Crime?' (2008) *9Canadian Military Journal* ,<http:www.journal.forces.gc.ca/vo9/no2/05-law;ess-eng.asp> accessed on 7 May 2013; See also Anthony d' Amato 'It's a Bird, It's a Plane, It's a Jus Cogens!' (1990) 6 *Connecticut Journal of International Law* 1.
77. Art. 51(2) of AP 1; Art. 33(1) of GC IV; Arts. 4(2)(d) and 13(2) of AP 2
78. *Galic* ICTY T. Ch. 30.11.2006 paras. 87-98. See Cryer, Friman...[et.al.], *An Introduction to International Criminal law and Procedure*, (2010).
79. Art. 4(d) of the ICTR Statute and Art. 3(d) of the SCSL Statute. See Harmen van der Wilt, Inez Braber, "The Case for Inclusion of terrorism in the Jurisdiction of the Criminal Court", *ACIL* Research Paper 2014-13, available at www.acil.uva.nl.
80. In *Galic* ICTY T. Ch. 5.12.2003
81. Cryer, Friman...[et.al.], *An Introduction to International Criminal law and Procedure*, (2010).
82. In *Galic* ICTY T. Ch. 5.12.2003
83. The evidence was submitted that civilians were attacked while attending funerals, while in ambulances and buses, while gardening and while shopping in markets.
84. See Robert Cryer, '*Prosecutor* v. *Galic* and the War Crime of Terror Bombing' (2005-2006) 2 *Israel Defence Force Law Review* 73; *Fofana and Kondewa* SCSL 28.5.2008 A. Ch. Paras 350-2.
85. Cryer, Friman...[et.al.], *An Introduction to International Criminal law and Procedure*, (2010). See alo Ben Saul, *Defining Terrorism in International Law* (OUP, Oxford 2006), Chapters 3-4.
86. Cryer, Friman...[et.al.], *An Introduction to International Criminal law and Procedure*, (2010).
87. *Galic* ICTY T. Ch. 5.12.2003. See also *Krstic* ICTY T. 12.8.2001 paras. 607, 653; *Prosecutor* v *Blagojevic*, par. 589.

88. This was substantiated by the International Law Commission which has resolved that 'the article (crimes against humanity, addition HvdW/IB) does not rule out the possibility that private individuals with de facto power or orgainsed in criminal gangs or groups might also commit the kind of systematic or mass violations of human rights covered by the article; in that case, their acts would come under the Draft Code'. Yearbook of the International Law Commission 1991, Volume 2, Part 2, part, A/CN.4/Ser.A/1991/Add.1 (part 2), p. 103.
89. See Antonio Cassese, 'Terrorism is also Disrupting Some Crucial Legal Categories of International Law' (2011) 12 *EJIL* 993 AT 994; See also Antonio Frederic Megret, 'Justice in Times of Violence' (2003) 14 *EJIL* 327 at 332-4.
90. See Roberta Arnold, 'Terrorism as a Crime Against Humanity under the ICC Statute' in Nesi, *International Cooperation in Counter-Terrorism*, 121; See William Schabas, 'Is Terrorism a Crime against Humanity?' (2002) 8 *International Peace keeping: The Yearbook of International Peace Operations* 225.
91. See Harmen van der Wilt, Inez Braber, "The Case for Inclusion of terrorism in the Jurisdiction of the Criminal Court", *ACIL* Research Paper 2014-13, available at www.acil.uva.nl. See also Clasuss Kress, 'On the Outer Limits of Crimes Against Humanity: The Concept of Organisation within the Policy requirement: Some Reflections on the March 2010 ICC Kenya Decision', *Leiden Journal of International Law* (2010), pp. 855-873.
92. Anderson, Perry (2001): 'Security Towards Bethlehem', *New Left Review*, 10 July/August; See also Roberta Arnold, The ICC as a New Instrument for Repressing Terrorism 56 (2004).
93. Aviv Cohen, Prosecuting Terrorists at the International Criminal Court: Reevaluating an Unused Legal Tool to Combat Terrorism, *Michigan State International Law Review*, Vol. 20: 2.
94. See George Fletcher, 'The Indefinable Concept of Terrorism', 4 *Journal of International Justice* (2006), pp. 902/903. See also M. Sassoli, 'Terrorism and War', 4 *Journal or International Justice* (2006), 979.

Chapter - 7

Human Rights and Terrorism

The violence and the fear perpetuated by terrorism is a common distressing feature of modern society. The alarming frequency of these terror acts is not only against the rights of the individual but also severely attacks the democratic government and institution. Numerous notorious incidents of terrorism around the world in recent past illustrates that terrorism remains an ongoing and severe threat to human rights of an individual and also a threat to regional and international peace and security. However, in the name of combating terrorism, several states are infringing the principles of human rights of innocent people. Such action of states is giving an excellent opportunity to these terrorist organisations to justify their menacing acts. Thus, if the democratic states want to combat terrorism, they have to do this without going against the principles of human rights, that is, without sacrificing fundamental freedom and dignity.

An inquiry into the origin, nature, and content of human rights is necessary in order to understand the relationship between human rights and terrorism.

Origin of Human Rights

The history of human rights is as old as civilisation itself. However, the modern international concern of human rights may be said to be comparatively of recent origin.[1] The nude dance of inhumanity, tyranny and complete massacre of law and order during the two World Wars compelled the world leaders to move forward in order to protect and promote the human rights for the welfare of humanity at large.[2] After the first World War efforts were made to incorporate specific provisions for human rights in the Covenant of League of Nations.[3] However, this world organisation failed to achieve the objects for which it was established.[4]

The World War II, above all things, illustrated specifically the close nexus between outrageous behaviour by the government of a country towards its own citizens and aggression against other countries, nexus between compliance of human rights and the maintenance of international peace and security.[5] It is, therefore, one of the main objects of the United Nations (UN) is to achieve international co-operation "in promoting and encouraging respect for human rights and fundamental freedoms for all without distinction as to race, sex, language or religion..." Reflecting this object, the UN Charter makes specific mention of human rights and fundamental freedoms in several clauses, viz. Articles 1, 13, 55, 56, 62, 68 and 76. These provisions were further elaborated through an International Bill of Rights.

As a part of International Bills of Rights, the Universal Declaration of Human Rights (UDHR) was adopted on 10 December 1948, "as a common standard of achievement for all peoples and all nations". The UDHR was followed by two international covenants, namely the International Covenant on Economic, Social and Cultural Rights (ICESCR) and the International Covenant on Civil and Political Rights (ICCPR) adopted and approved by the General Assembly in 1966.[6] At present, several conventions are dealing with the subject of human rights.[7]

The international legal regime of human rights has undergone a sea change after the Second World War.[8] The growth of legal regime concerning human rights is well-described by Louis Henkin.[9] According to him, "The UN Charter ushered in a new international law of human rights. The new law buried the old dogma that the individual is not a 'subject' of international politics and law and that a government's behaviour toward its own nationals is a matter of domestic, and international concern...It gave the individual a part in international politics and rights in international law, independently of his government.

It also gave the individual protectors other than his government, indeed protectors and remedies against his government."[10]

In the long process evolution, modern human rights jurisprudence has been crystallised into three basic principles.[11] First, the principle of universal inherence, which provides that every human being has certain rights, capable of being enumerated and defined which are not conferred on him by any ruler, nor earned or acquired by purchase, they by virtue of their being human possess these rights; second, the principle of inalienability, according to this principle, no human being shall be deprived of any of those certain fundamental rights by the acts of ruler or even by his own act or in a democracy even by the will of the majority of the sovereign people; and third, the rule of law, as per this principle, in case of conflict of interests, such conflict must be determined by the consistent, independent and impartial application of just laws under just procedures.

The contemporary approach of human rights is demonstrated in the World Conference on Human Rights, 1993 popularly known as the Vienna Declaration. The Declaration states explicitly that all human rights are universal, indivisible and interdependent and interrelated and that democracy, development, human rights and fundamental freedom are mutually interdependent. In this reference Vienna Declaration observed that: "While the significance of national and regional particularities and various historical, cultural and religious backgrounds must be borne in mind, it is the duty of States, regardless of their political, economic and cultural systems, to promote and protect all human rights and fundamental freedoms."[12]

Classification of Human Rights

Human rights have evolved and developed as a reaction to oppressive institutions, policies and practices. The generation of human rights is discerned to be responses to the economic and political oppression that was the by-product of colonialism and industrial capitalism.[13] The proponent of the classification of rights into three generations was Karl Vasek, a former Director of the Human Rights and Peace Division of the United Nations Educational, Scientific and Cultural Organisation (UNESCO)[14].

The division follows the three significant watchwords of the French Revolution: *Liberte, Egalite, Fraternite.* The first-generation human rights deal primarily with liberty. They are fundamentally civil and political rights serve to protect the individual from the excesses of the state. The first generation rights are mostly negative rights, and these are first enforced at the international platform by the Universal Declaration of Human Rights, 1948. Articles 3 to 21 of the UDHR and the International Covenant on Civil and Political Rights comes under this division.[15]

The second generation of human rights relates to equality. They are primarily social, economic and cultural rights. In a social context, they ensure different members of the citizenry equal conditions and treatment. These are mostly positive rights, representing things that the state is required to provide to the people under its jurisdiction.[16] Articles 22 to 27 of the Universal Declaration of Human rights, and the International Covenant of Economic and Social Rights. According to Szabo, there is need for an approach which harmonises the first and second generations of human rights, because the purpose of human rights is to defend by institutionalised means the rights of human being against abuses of power committed by the organs of the state and, at the same time, to promote the multi-dimensional development of the human personality.[17]

The third-generation human rights focus basically on fraternity and, also called as solidarity rights.[18] They cover six solidarity rights; three reflect the emergence of third world nationalism and, it asserts for a global redistribution of power, wealth and other important values. The six solidarity rights covered under the third generation of human rights are as follows: (1) The right to political, social, economic, and cultural self-determination; (2) The right to social and economic development; (3) The right to participate and to be benefitted from the common heritage of humanity; (4) The right to peace; (5) The right to healthy and balanced environment; and (6) The right to humanitarian disaster relief.[19]

In brief, it can be said that the first generation rights are related to liberty; the second generation rights to equality and the third generation rights are related to fraternity.

Universality of Human Rights

The universality of human rights is often debated and challenged. It is usually referred to as a 'North-South' divide by states that seek to emphasise one set of rights over another.[20] Cultural relativists are of the view that while in the west an individual and his/ her rights are considered above the group rights, however, this is not universally applicable and that certain societies of the South are ordered on the lines of the community.[21] For example, some nations have recorded reservations against specific provisions of the Convention on the Elimination of Discrimination against Women (CEDAW). Several Islamic nations have objection on the provisions enshrined in CEDAW on the ground that it conflicts with the Islamic Shariah system of law.[22] The enforcement of rights under conventions is often impaired by sovereign nations claiming that purported universal rights conflict with their cultures.

Further, the various advancements and positive effects of human rights face challenges in their implementations.[23] However, the concept of human rights is universal in nature since they apply to every human in every society without discrimination. Human rights are considered to be inalienable as they emerge from nature to protect and develop the human condition; they cannot be snatched away by anyone without jeopardising the value of the existence of the rights. However, the universal and inalienable characteristics of human rights are debatable in both their perception and implementation.[24]

To a certain extent, the universality of human rights depends upon their genesis. Human rights may come into existence in two ways, they may be created by the people in the society, and the other way is to discover it in the society.[25] If human rights are simply inventions, then it is rather difficult to argue that every society and government should bound by something with which they disagree. However, if human rights have an existence independent of human creation, then in such a case, it is easier to assert their universality. However, such independent moral standards may be established in only two way, one, if God creates them, and two, if such rights are natural and innate to mankind and society.[26]

It is not only the genesis or origin of the human rights which presents the challenge to the universal nature of human rights but also the lack of inspiration in implementation of human rights by the people in a given society. Everyone will not agree that everything asserted as human rights is indeed one. At a very to primary level, the proclamation and the acceptance of the human right norms inherently involves the acceptance of the majority of the people in the society.[27] Individual right exists because a majority of the section of people approves it. However, on the other hand, minorities who object the concept of human rights, have rejected the idea that particular right is an essential need of humans, as well as the relationship between individuals and their community.[28] Complex issues/ problems arise when there is a dispute between conflicting spiritual and temporal values within or between societies. The difficulties come to the forefront when one tries to ascertain whether human rights can set global standards on the treatment that must be given to all human beings[29].

However, the adoption of Vienna Declaration 1993, demonstrates that there are few if any, human rights issues today, which are not of international concern. It is in this context that the statement in Paragraph 4 of the Declaration that "the promotion and protection of all human rights is a legitimate concern of the international community."[30] The similar idea also finds expression in another, equally important principle proclaimed in the Vienna Declaration. Paragraph 5 of the Declaration provides that, "All human rights are universal, indivisible, and interdependent and interrelated. The international community must treat human rights globally in a fair and equal manner, on the same footing, and with the same emphasis. While the significance of national and regional particularities and various historical, cultural and religious backgrounds must be born in mind, it is the duty of the states, regardless of their political, economic and cultural systems, to promote and protect all human rights and fundamental freedoms."[31]

The recognition of the universal character of human rights and the concomitant rejection of cultural relativism, which has traditionally sought to justify violations of human rights by reference to some particular religious or cultural imperatives, laid the foundation for global effort to improve the human rights situation of all human beings.

Human Rights Dimensions of Terrorism

The direct relation between terrorism and violation of human rights was recognised by the World Conference on Human Rights (Vienna,

1993) of the Vienna Declaration and its Programme of Action which stipulated that "the acts, methods and practices of terrorism in all its forms and manifestations as well as linking it to drug trafficking are activities purports to the violation of human rights, fundamental freedoms and other democracy, threatening territorial integrity, security of states and destabilising legitimately constituted Government."[32]

The growing consciousness of international community of the adverse effects of terrorism in all its forms on the full enjoyment of the human rights, fundamental freedoms, on the establishment of the Rule of Law and democratic freedoms as enshrined in the UN Charter and the international covenants on human rights. All states are required to suppress all or any form of terrorist activities within their borders as terrorism represented the globalization of fear and contempt for the role of international law.

It was for the first time in the UN history that 168 member states participated in the discussion of a single agenda item on international terrorism, which started on 1st October 2001. This demonstrates the seriousness of the International Community that regarded acts of terrorism as assaults on civilisation itself. The dangerous trend towards an expansion of the scope of the terrorist had turned it into a real and apparent threat to humanity.

According to Wilkson, it is interesting to note that the concept of terrorism and human rights have some characteristic features in common. Terrorism, as well as human rights, entered into the political discourse roughly at the time of the French Revolution. Edmund Burke's sensitive denunciation of the Jacobin reign of terror in his "Reflection of the French Revolution" and his opponent Thomas Paine's equally impassioned contention "The right of Man" helped to bring these concepts into English political dictionary. Terrorism and human rights are vigorously debated concepts from the beginning. Consequently, both these concepts are indispensable part of modern moral and political vocabulary.[33]

However, the similarities between the concept of terrorism and human rights do not go further and end there, except in cases where one argues that there is an inherent human right to blow up or shoot fellow human beings or to hold them hostages or to terrorise them by any other means, nevertheless, such acts, as mentioned, is a threat to human rights.[34]

In considering the human rights dimensions of terrorism, it is not only the number of victims that should be taken into consideration but also its impact on the victims, the society and the state. Killing hundreds of innocent people, destroying their property and creating an atmosphere of fear and terror in the minds of the people in a society infringes the human rights of the people living in a society.

Terrorism: A Human Right Violation

Generally, it is regarded that the states are the guarantors, protectors and violators of human rights. The term terrorism is generally understood as an unlawful, co-coordinated, politically motivated violence against 'innocents' or 'civilians' with the effect of terrorising the population and non-state actors generally practise unlawful co-coordinated, politically motivated violence. However, the state, too in some instances practices terrorism, but its act usually fits into the well-established framework of human rights and humanitarian law.[35]

Terrorist activities are generally considered to be a crime. However, such acts of terror are not considered as a human rights violation, notwithstanding the heinous nature of the terrorist act. However, it is undebatable, that acts of terror have severe and damaging effects on human rights, beyond the loss of life, injury and torture that are immediate products of terrorist attacks; there exist the web of other rights that are disregarded. Terrorism, generally affects the economy of the state, either through discouraging trade and investment or shifting the state resources to counter-terrorism measures.

Consequently, economic and social rights, such as health care and education, are affected. Civil and Political rights, such as privacy and security, may be abridged. The exercise of freedom of speech may be inhibited or repressed in an atmosphere of crisis, and intolerance of groups associated with the enemy may flourish, sometimes reaching the level of violent reprisal.[36]

Another facet of the nexus between human rights and terrorism is the motivational factor which motivates the person to practice terrorism. The state violation of human rights can degrade social norms more generally, terrorists time to time attempt to justify their acts as a lawful means to accomplish or achieve protection and benefits provided by human rights standards for themselves or others in their communities.[37] In other words, terrorists demand the authority of the rule of law to legitimise human rights protections or benefits and argue that their acts are a legitimate means to achieve redress of these demands. Thus, in many cases, measures of state repression can also promote militancy in public, swelling ranks of terrorist recruits.[38]

State Responses to Terrorism & Impact on Human Rights

Undoubtedly, terrorist acts violate human rights. However, it is unequivocally true that harsh responses of the states in countering the menace of terrorism have a degrading effect, though sometimes less visible. The impact of any given terrorist act is usually limited in time, but restrictive and severe state responses may have a long duration impact and affect the lives of many more people than the terror attacks. The impact of restrictive measures may include the arbitrary deprivation of life or liberty, curtailment of due process guarantees, privacy incursions, limits on speech, and restrictions on the rights of aliens, among others.

Many leaders without wasting any time justified questionable policies in terms of the Sept 11 attack. Arial Sharon designated Yassir Arafat as "our bin Laden." China termed, peaceful and insurrectionist Uighur separatists, in Xinjiang's as 'terrorist.' Once the United States Government-linked a particular Muslim organisation to the Al-Qaeda network, Uzbek President Islam Kasimov used this act to further justify his Government's crackdown on peaceful believers in the name of counter-terrorism[39].

Many nations which are already saddled with the worst human rights records in the region, in the name of counter-terrorism policy opened new doors to further curb down the freedom of expression and privacy and other human rights. The state authorities in the name of combating terrorism misused their powers for their benefits or purposes and, thus, violated the rights of others, as they are exempted from damages for inflicting harm during counter-terrorism operation and are authorised to harm the lives, health and property of terrorists.[40]

Several countries enacted laws that restrict and violate human rights, in the name of the 'War on Terror.' One need not have to go further to find such questionable counter-terrorism. India, one of the world's largest democracies, enacted two specific anti-terrorist laws one Terrorist and Disruptive Activities (Prevention) Act, 1987 (TADA) and the second one was Prevention of Terrorism Act, 2001 (POTA). These two laws were known for its harsh and draconian features and which were also in contravention with the well-established tenets of Criminal Justice System founded on Rule of Law. These two draconian laws from the statute book of the largest democracy straightway were in confrontation with the fundamental human rights, some of which are enshrined in Part III of the Constitution of India.

The obnoxious provisions of TADA and POTA had been adversely criticised. TADA and POTA were found to have been involved more often in states not affected by terrorism. Innocent people were detained, harassed due to extensive abuse of these two anti-terrorist laws. Only a few of the accused were convicted under the due process of law. Both these anti-terrorism laws were used as a tool to fight trade unions and to detain Muslims, Sikhs, Dalits, and political opponents. The Supreme Court of India, observing the misuse of the anti-terrorism laws observed that "when the law visits a person with serious penal consequences extra care and precaution must be taken to ensure that those whom the legislature did not intend to be covered by the express language of the statue are not to be roped in by stretching the language of the law."[41]

A draconian anti-terrorism law was also enacted in Britain without any proper parliamentary scrutiny. The Anti-Terrorism, Crime and Security Act which had the same aim as the United States Patriot Act. This Act authorised the indefinite detention of a suspect without trial - internment by another name - on people of other jurisdictions whom the Home Secretary 'reasonably' believes are terrorists or have links with an international terrorist group or are 'a risk' to national security. 'Terrorism' is defined in the Act covering 'the use or threat of action' designed to influence the government or to advance a 'political', religious or ideological cause'. Further, such action includes the threat of committing 'serious damage to property.'[42] To combat terrorism, the British government suspended its obligations under the European

Convention on Human Rights and the United Nation's International Covenant on Civil and Political Rights. Which gave way to the British authorities to detain any person for an indefinite period. It was viewed by The Sunday Observer of London on March 10, 2002, described such harsh provision and stated: "we do not lack legal powers to tackle terrorism. The new power is merely to imprison people where there is no quality evidence that they have committed any crime.'[43]

United Nations senior officials realised the facts that the Security Council Resolution 1373 of September 28 was being misused by some member states to justify repression of domestic dissent. Bacre Waly Ndiaye, the Chief Human Rights officer at United Nations Secretariat, informed the Council's new Counter-Terrorism Committee, that: "There is evidence that some countries are now introducing measures that may erode human rights safeguards." In several countries, Ndiaye informed the committee at its December 13, 2001, meeting that "non-violent activities are also considered as terrorism, and excessive steps are taken by the governments to suppress and restrict individual fundamental rights including the presumption of innocence, the right to a fair trial, freedom from torture, privacy rights, freedom of expression and assembly and right to seek asylum.[44]

However, the following are the primary rights among others which are violated by terrorists or by state while fighting against them.

Right to Life

A welfare and democratic state must protect the right to life of every person. However, the large number of innocent people are killed, massacred and maimed by terrorism in indiscriminate and random acts of violence and terror. Such terror acts cannot be justified under any circumstances. The terrorist attacks all over the world targeted innocent people and created fear among the general public and, no cause could justify such cowardly and murderous actions. It creates an environment that destroys the right to be free from fear and the right to live in peace.[45]

Moreover, the states by overreacting and attacking terrorists without thinking of the consequences are also violating human rights. Such a senseless retaliation by the powerful nations such as the United

States, Russia etc., plunged the entire Afghanistan, Iraq and Syria into great suffering, pain and insecurity making the poor civilian lose their shelter, their belongings and their livelihood for no fault but the fault of few terrorist organisations such as al-Qaida and Islamic State.[46]

Right to Religion

At present, the world has assumed the status of the global village, which is multi-cultural and multi-religious in nature. After September 11th attack in the United States, the concept of global village was shaken, and the world was divided into two parts; Islam was at one side while rests on the other; all Muslims were looked upon with suspicion as having links with terrorists and terrorism and they became the unwanted species in the western world and were seen with hatred.[47] Any attempt to identify or equate the fight against terrorism with one religion, race or country defeat its purpose in ensuring peace and security, building tolerance, safeguarding multiculturalism and avoiding fragmentation.

The Permanent Observer of the Islamic Conference emphasised the fact that Islam was opposed to all forms of violence and terrorism as well as against intolerance, aggression or acts that violated the rights of people and their property. It was also reported that some Muslims living in the United States are anglicising their Arabic origin names to escape harassment and suspicion which in-fact deprives them of their right to name, Sikhs were also targeted for wearing a turban-like Osama. The cold-hearted and promiscuous killing of innocent people in Sri Lanka is a crime against humanity and religion.[48]

Rights of Migrants

Migrants are a particularly vulnerable group, and they find their rights routinely violated. In order to eliminate widespread discrimination against the migrant workers and members of their families a Convention was adopted by the General Assembly on December 18, 1990 (General Assembly Resolution 45/158, dated December 18, 1990) which is known as the International Convention on the Protection of the Rights of All Migrant Workers and Members of their Family.[49]

The migrants, who always find a difficult time to adapt themselves to new surroundings and societies, quite often face discrimination in their efforts to integrate into their new countries. Moreover, they are seen unjustifiably, as potential enemies and looked upon with suspicion. There was a potential change in the attitude of the people, in the manner they think and interact with each other and the immediate effect had been on the way immigrants were being perceived by many individuals and societies. The third committee of the 59th General Assembly during its 39th meeting held on 13th November 20021 was informed that situations of Migrants become more difficult since the 11th September attack.[50]

Right to Development

Right to development is considered to be the third generation right. There could be no development and progress without the existence of peace, especially in today's globalised world. Destabilising legitimately constituted governments, underestimating pluralistic civil society and Rule of Law have adverse consequences on the economic, social and political development of a country, which also took the form of attacks against the tourist industry.[51]

Apart from violations of these significant human rights, concerns have arisen for right against torture, arbitrary detention (The United States had detained hundreds of people at Guantanamo Bay) and denial of a fair trial (The United States had used a system of military commissions to try terror suspects, which do not offer the fundamental guarantees of a fair trial. Further countries like India and the United Kingdom have had enacted a particular procedure for trying terror suspects). The use of enhanced interrogations techniques, extraordinary renditions and the widespread use of diplomatic assurances have also led to violation of inalienable human rights.[52]

No Clash Between Human Rights and Combating Terrorism

The impossibility of trying to restrain terrorism while not jeopardising human rights, to some extent cannot be denied but then in a country that craves strength, order and stability, and believes that only laws provide them, while it remembers anxiously, paranoically, the past, we cannot afford to give in to any kind to hysteria when the very liberty is at stake.

In Rex *v* Halliday[53] Lord Atkinson observed as follows: "However precious the personal liberty of the subject may be, there is something for which it may be, to some extent, sacrificed by legal enactment, namely, national success in war, or escape from national plunder or enslavement."[54]

However, it must be kept in mind that, the higher the power, the more dangerous the abuse. Burke expressed his fear more than two and a half centuries ago in his letter to the Hon'ble Chief Justice Fox (8 October 1777), "People crushed by law have no hopes but from power. If laws are their enemies, they will be enemies to laws; and those, who have much hope and nothing to lose, will always be dangerous, more or less."[55]

So the approach has to be cautious and only those roped in who could be termed, terrorists. The harassment and sacrifice of the liberty of the innocents in the name of prevention of terrorist activities is inadmissible.

Justice Mathew in Prabhu Dayal Deorath etc. *v* The District Magistrate, Kamrup and others[56], while delivering the majority judgment emphasised the preservation of personal liberty and expressed his views that: "We say, and we think it is necessary to repeat, that gravity of the evil to the community resulting from the antisocial activities can never furnish an adequate reason for evading the personal liberty of a citizen, except by the procedure established by the constitution and the laws. The history of personal liberty is largely the history of insistence on observance of procedure. Observance of the procedure has been a bastion against wanton assaults on personal liberty over the years under our Constitution, the only guarantee of personal liberty for a person is that he shall not be deprived of it except by the procedure established by law."[57]

Generally, it is debated that without infringing human rights, the war against terrorism cannot be won. However, there is no such conflict between these two highly debated concepts. International humanitarian law is an indispensable branch of human rights law implemented even in a situation of armed conflict. However, there is a continuing confluence between the two as the aim of both is the same, that is, to regard human rights and dignity as well as to abjure needless violence.

The fundamental concepts of laws of war are based on the balance between military necessity and humanity which includes proportionality of the force used. Military necessity does not admit cruelty or wounding in fight against terror. Geneva Conventions lays down the provisions for humane treatment even of the prisoner of wars. Therefore, the action of the party during conflict has to be governed by the Geneva convention. Thus, if humane considerations prevail in armed conflict with an enemy, the treatment of persons dealt with in low-intensity conflict cannot be harsher because they are often not the enemies of the nations. The entire framework of Hague laws and Geneva laws encompasses the area and there is a growing convergence between them.[58]

Human rights advocates argue that the role of human rights protection is an inseparable part to fight against the menace of terrorism. This suggests that respecting the rights of an individual and his dignity may actually assist the state in achieving peace and security. Amnesty International included a section on confronting terrorism in the recommendations in the Madrid Agenda arising from the Madrid Summit on Democracy and Terrorism (Madrid, 8-11 March 2005): "Democracy principles and values are essential tools in the fight against terrorism. Any successful strategy for dealing with terrorism requires terrorists to be isolated. Consequently, the preference must be to treat terrorism as criminal acts to be handled through existing systems of law enforcement and with full respect for human rights and the rule of law.[59]

The promotion and development of freedom and human dignity through effective democracy is the long-term solution for winning the war against terrorism. Effective democracies honour and uphold fundamental human rights, such as freedom of speech and expression, press, assembly, association, and religion etc. are responsive towards their citizens and regards the will of the people.Such democratic states also limit the spectrum of governance and protect the institution of civil society. Such democratic states exercise effective sovereignty and maintain order within their jurisdictional boundaries; tackle causes of conflict in a peaceful manner, protect independent and impartial systems of justice, punish crime, embrace the rule of law, and resist corruption.

In such democracies, freedom is indivisible. Moreover, they are the long-term antidote to the ideology of terrorism today.[60]

Defending human rights is a prerequisite to every aspect of any effective counter-terrorism strategy. It is a bond that brings the different components together. That means the human rights of all—of the victims of the terror act, suspects of terrorism, of those affected by the consequences of the terrorism.[61] A person who respects human rights cannot support terrorism which is a severe violation of human rights. Thus, there is no conflict between respect for human rights and combating terrorism. Ms Mary Robison, the United Nations High Commissioner for Human Rights, emphasised that "the government efforts must be within the sphere of human rights principles, which maintains a right equilibrium between enjoyment of rights and freedom and a balance between the enjoyment of freedoms and the justifiable concern for national security."[62]

While fighting with the menace of terrorism, the international community must support and endorse the statement of the former UN Secretary-General Kofi Annan that: "... we shall find that human rights, along with democracy and social justice are one of the best prophylactics against terrorism and that in combating terrorism it will be self-defeating it we sacrifice other key priorities such as human rights in the process."[63] No doubt, terrorism is the gravest problem, but we cannot afford to take any action in haste when human rights are at stake. Human rights, democracy and the rule of law are the most solid foundations for stability of peace. In this regard, it would be significant to quote Ms Mary Robinson, former High Commissioner for Human Rights in her report at the 58th session of the United Nations Commission for Human Rights, where she stressed that: "There should be three guiding principles for the world community: the need to eliminate discrimination and build a just and tolerant world; the cooperation by all states against terrorism, without using such cooperation as a pretext to infringe on Human rights; and a strong commitment to the rule of law"[64].

Further Ms Mary Robinson speaking on War against Terrorism said: "...At the same time, building durable global human rights culture, by asserting the value and worth of every human being, is essential if terrorism is to be eliminated. In other words, the promotion of human rights should be at the centre of the strategy to counter terrorism...what must never be forgotten is that human rights are no hindrances to the promotions of peace and security rather they are an essential element of any strategy to defeat terrorism ."[65]

Notes

1. See, Micheline.R. Ishay, *The History of Human Rights: From Ancient Times to the globalisation Era* (2004); Jeffrey Kahn, "Protection and Empire: The Martens Clause, State Sovereignity, and Individual Rights", 56(1) *Virginia Journal of International law* (2016), pp. 1-49; S. Fredman, *Human Rights Transformed: Positive Rights and Positive Duties* (2018)
2. Eleanor Roosevelt, "The Struggle for Human Rights," *Department of State Bulletin* (10 October 1948), pp. 457-466.
3. See, Micheline.R. Ishay, *The History of Human Rights: From Ancient Times to the globalisation Era* (2004).
4. F S Northedge, *The League of nations: Its Life and Times, 1920-1946* (1986).
5. See, Philip Alston and Euan MacDonald, *Human Rights, Intervention, and Use of Force*, (2008). See also, SIRACUSA PRINCIPLES on the Limitation and Derogation https://www.icj.org/wp-content/uploads/1984/07/Siracusa-principles-ICCPR-legal-submission-1985-eng.pdf
6. See, T. Buergenthal, "The Normative and Intuitional Evolution of International Human Rights," 19(4), *Human Rights Quarterly* (1987), pp. 703-723.
7. See, Claire Than and Edwin Shorts, *International Criminal Law and Human Rights*, (Sweet & Maxwell, 2003)
8. See, Micheline.R. Ishay, *The History of Human Rights: From Ancient Times to the globalisation Era* (2004).
9. L. Henkin (Ed.) *The International Bill of Rights: The Covenant on Civil and political Rights* (1981), p. 6.
10. *Ibid.*
11. N.K.Jayakumar, *International Law and Human Rights*, (2005), p. 332.
12. See, Vienna Declaration and Prrgramme of Action, as adopted by the World Conference on Human Rights on 25 June 1993, UN Doc. A/Conf.157/23 9 (12 July 1993), para 5.
13. See, The Vienna Declaration And Programme of Action, World Conference on Human Rights, Vienna, 14-25 June 1993, at http://www.unhchr.ch/huridocda/huridoca.nsf/(symbole)/; See, E.S. Venkataramiah, "Human Rights in the Changing World" in E.S. Venkataramiah (Ed.) *Emerging Human Rights* (1988)
14. Morton Winston, 'On the Indivisibility and Interdependence of Human Rights', at http://www.bu.edu/wcp/papers/huma/humaWins.htm.
15. See, Domaradzki, S., Khvostova, M. & Pupovac, D. *Hum Rights Rev* (2019) 20: 423. https://doi.org/10.1007/s12142-019-00565-x
16. *Ibid.*

17. See Louis B. Sohan: "The International Law: Protection of the Rights of Individuals Rather than states" 32 *Am. U.L. Rev.* 1 (1982) reprinted in Thomas Buergenthal and Dinah Shelton, pp. 9-17.
18. See, R. Freedman, "Third Generation Rights: Is there Room for Hybrid Constructs within International Human Rights Law?" 2(4), *Cambridge Journal of International and Comparative law.*
19. Stephen marks, "The Human Right to Development: Between Rhetoric and Reality" 17 *Harvard Human Rights Journal* (2004), pp. 136-168.
20. See, Andrew Clapham, *Human Rights: A Very Short Introduction*, (2105)
21. Amy Eckert, "Universality by Consensus: The Evolution of Universality in the Drafting of the UDHR, A Review to The Universal Declaration of Human Rights: Drafting, Origin and Intent by Johannes Morsink,'"Philadelphia: University of Pennsylvania Press, 2000, Pennsylavania Studies in Human Rights, at http://www.du.edu/gsis/hrhw/volumes/2001/1-2/morsink-eckert.pdf. Accessed on 2 May 2019.
22. Report of the Committee on the Elimination of All Forms of Discrimination against Women on Reservations to the Convention on the Elimination of All Forms of Discrimination against Women, at http://www.un.org/documents/ga/cedaw/16/cedawc1997-4.htm. Accessed on 3 May 2019.
23. See, Andrew Clapham, *Human Rights: A Very Short Introduction*, (2105)
24. *Ibid.*
25. Andrew Heard, "Introduction to Human Rights Theories- Human Rights: Chimeras in Sheep's Clothing", at http://www.sfu.ca/~aheard/intro.html. Accessed on 23 May 2019.
26. *Ibid.*
27. *Ibid.*
28. *Ibid.*
29. *Ibid.*
30. Thomas Buerganthal, "International Human Rights in an Historical Perspective", Janusz Symonides (ed.) *Human Rights Concepts and Standards*, (2002), p. 16.
31. *Ibid.*
32. The Viena Declaration and Programme of Action, World Conference on Human Rights, Vienna, 14-25 June 1993, at http://www.unhchr.ch/huridocda/. Accessed on 25 November 2019.
33. See, Paul Wilkson, "Terrorism and Human Rights", at www.st-andrews.ac.uk/intrel/research/cstpv/journals/articles/commonwealthministersreferencebook2007.pdf. Accessed on 7 June 2019.
34. *Ibid.*
35. See, Fotion, Kashnikov & Lekea, *Terrorism: The New World Disorder*, (Continuum International, 2008)
36. Human Rights Watch, "We are not enemy: Hate Crimes against Arabs, Muslims, and Those Perceived to be Arabs or Muslims, After September 11". In a Short Human Rights Watch Report, Vol. 14, No. 6, Nov. 2002, at http://www.hrw.org/reports/2002/usahate/usa1102.pdf. Accessed on 4 July 2019.

37. Defense Institute of International Legal Studies: Human Rights and Terrorism, at http://www.dsca.mil/Diils/251%20Human%20Rights%20and%20Terrorism%20.pdf. Accessed on 24 January 2019
38. *Ibid.*
39. "Opportunism in the Face of Tragedy: Repression in the name of Anti-terrorism", at http://hrw.org/campaigns/september11/opportunismwatch.htm, Accessed on 12 May 2019.
40. *Ibid.*
41. Niranjan Singh Karam Singh Panjabi V Jintendra Bhimraj (1990) 4SCC 76: Kartar Singh V State of Punjab (1994) 3SCC 569.
42. Ninan Koshy, *The War on Terror,* (2003), p.93; See also, David J. Whittaker, *Counter-Terrorism and Human Rights,* (2009)
43. *Ibid.*
44. *Ibid.*
45. See, David J. Whittaker, *Counter-Terrorism and Human Rights,* (2009)
46. See, Claire Than and Edwin Shorts, *International Criminal Law and Human Rights*, (Sweet & Maxwell, 2003)
47. See, David J. Whittaker, *Counter-Terrorism and Human Rights,* (Pearson, 2009)
48. Y. Lakshmi G. Rao, "Terrorism and its impact on Human Rights", *A.I.R Journal* (2002) p183-187; See also, S K Desai, *Terrorism: New Political Religions*, (2012)
49. See, Claire Than and Edwin Shorts, *International Criminal Law and Human Rights*, (Sweet & Maxwell, 2003)
50. Y. Lakshmi G. Rao, "Terrorism and its impact on Human Rights", A.I.R Journal (2002) p183-187; See also, , Claire Than and Edwin Shorts, *International Criminal Law and Human Rights*, (2003); David J. Whittaker, *Counter-Terrorism and Human Rights,* (2009)
51. *Ibid.*
52. *Ibid.*
53. [1917 A.C. 260 (269)]
54. R. Swaroop, *Cases and Material on TADA*, (1993), p. 5.
55. *Ibid.,* p.9
56. 1974 (2) SCR 12 (22)
57. *Ibid.*
58. J.S.Verma, *The New Universe of Human Rights*, (2004) p. 107.
59. Maj. Gen. R S Mehta (ed.), *International Encyclopaedia of Terrorism Laws*, (2007), p. 127.
60. *Ibid.,* p. 684.
61. *Ibid.,* p. 156.
62. J.S.Verma, *The New Universe of Human Rights*, (2004) p. 107.
63. R.K. Pradhan, *Terrorism Rule of Law and Human Rights*, (1st ed. 2010); A. Subbian, *Human Rights and Human Rights*, (1st ed. 2005).

64. See Introductory Statement by Mary Robinson, United Nations High Commissioner for Human Rights, COMMISSION ON HUMAN RIGHTS, *Annual Report*, 58th session, (March 20, 2003), http://www.unhchr.ch. (last updated November 10, 2007); J.S. Verma, *The New Universe of Human Rights* 108 (1st ed. 2002).
65. *Ibid.*

Index

J

K

R

S